PARANOIA

EXTINCTION-CLASS INCIDENT RESPONSE

Mission Leader
W. J. MACGUFFIN

Written by
WJ MACGUFFIN, JAIME BREWER, JASON BRICK AND STEPHEN WHITEHEAD

Grand Overseer
GARETH HANRAHAN

WORD WRANGLER
MATTHEW SPRANGE

Paranoia created by
DAN GELBER, GREG COSTIKYAN AND ERIC GOLDBERG

COVER ART
Cassie Gregory

Graphic design and artwork by
Cassie Gregory and Amy Perrett

PROOFREADING: Charlotte Law

HEROES OF ALPHA COMPLEX: Roger Howe, Leigh Keegan, MacLaren North % Extent, Kevin Fritzke, Brian Davis, Oliver Lauenstein, Omer Raviv, Nozomi Oguma, Ron Dautzenberg, Jason Winstanley, Ian Newborn, Adam Longley, Steve Weaver, James Petts, James C Napier IV, Nathan Bowerbank, Eric Brooke, Kyle Jerviss, Michael Nason, Boyd Ridley Critz, Chris Kuivenhoven, Anthony Pirri, Robert Haubenstricker, John Weaver, Frank Forte, Matt Selter, Bradford Kobryn, Chris Mitchell, Lyle Hayhurst, Aaron M. Grayson, Rianna Preston, Joseph Yoblonski, Matthew D Rose, Aisling Jensen, Eric K Sigler, Jesse Butler, David Armand, Ken Smith, John F. Schank III, Adam Starkweather, Charles Reed, John J Senn, Tyler Beck, Jamie Law, Michael Salas, Chuck Barbee

GENTLEMAN TONE CZAR: Ken Rolston

ATTENTION: THIS IS CLASSIFIED FOR THE GM ONLY
PLAYERS SHOULD WALK AWAY BRISKLY BUT WITHOUT PANICKING

CONTENTS

EXTINCTION-CLASS INCIDENT RESPONSE

An R&D report on experiments that could have destroyed all that we know and love but did not[1].

Complied by R&D with support from all Service Groups working together in harmony and efficiency like they always do, Year 214.

HEY, SHE ASKED FOR EVERYTHING WE HAD IN STOCK.

R&D experiments are necessary to provide cutting-edge research into fighting terrorists and protecting The Computer, Alpha Complex and its citizens (in that order). However, there are times[2] when such experiments produce unintended and catastrophic results[3]. When these threaten our very existence, including and especially The Computer, a detailed response is needed to prevent an extinction-class event[4].

In response to a Computer request[5], R&D created an Extinction-Class Incident Response Team (ECIRT) with experts[6] from all Service Groups. Working together occasionally, the ECIRT created reports to evaluate responses as well as the experiments themselves in order to prevent any accidental apocalypse that could make The Computer feel lonely.

[1] A report on experiments that did destroy all that we know and love is forthcoming.
[2] R&D assures everyone this is very, very rare. Yes, they wanted us to print 'very' twice.
[3] Past catastrophes are not a predictor of future results, so get off R&D's back already.
[4] These are events that could lead to the extinction of all humanity, so it is kinda a big deal.
[5] Sure. 'Request'. Very funny.
[6] Each Service Group defined 'expert' differently, so this is going to be a hot mess.

How can this help your *Paranoia* missions become even more fun and deadly? These 15 reports describe a fascinating way multiple apocalypses (apocali?) just about happened in Alpha Complex but did not thanks to hard work, sheer luck and judicious use of summary executions.

But these are not just some light reading and not just because they are rather dark at times. They come with a three-act mission prompt related to the armageddons (armageddi?) in question. If you want to run *Paranoia* and need some ideas to kickstart your creative juices (juici?), now you have 15 of 'em, all hand-crafted using artisanal laptops and locally-sourced insanity to delight the senses, tickle the palette and make sure Troubleshooters die like fools they are.

BIOSYN

TROUBLESHOOTER SMASH!

EXECUTIVE SUMMARY

Citizens depend on The Computer to offer medication cocktails* for happiness, clearance-relative health and the occasional relief from mind-numbing boredom. While modifications to the cocktail are possible, this is difficult to alter without more unwanted side effects. Few clones can pronounce drug names, never mind have the Security Clearance to work with biochemical models. Recently, R&D authorised the creation of a new team of biotech scientists who really needed a promotion and some very high Mystics from across Alpha Complex to pursue the issue. R&D Team Dry Mouth showed 13% more than the expected zeal for a task known to yield low success and little recognition.

Statherosynigeraline, short name BioSyn, was the most promising candidate to come out of Team Dry Mouth and was approved for trials. It yielded a small but significant reduction in overall side effects, with only mutants experiencing a workplace performance issue (this was verified by testing on registered mutants; non-registered mutants uncovered due to the trial were subsequently terminated). The drug was deemed safe for wider testing based on current IntSec statistics on mutations within the population. Those figures are in the process of being revised. When introduced to the wider population, it gave rise to a variety of random and dangerous Mutant Powers that spun out of control.

As of this writing, all data pertaining to BioSyn has been reclassified Violet clearance and possession of the drug (or data that could lead to it being recreated) are punishable with at least summary execution and erasure of DNA template. Efforts are underway to dissolve Team Dry Mouth pending acquisition of enough sulphuric acid.

[1] For those of Blue clearance and higher, this is not a drink like the Sideautocar or Teela Fizz.

MATERIALS and METHODOLOGY
To formulate BioSyn, Team Dry Mouth hit upon the tried-and-true method of 'try drugs randomly and see what works because hey I'm not taking any'. A large volume of Infrared test subjects were available courtesy of the recent IntSec 'Volunteer Your Neighbour for XP Points!' campaign. No single medication had a positive effect on side effects more than 4%. Doing some quick math, the team realised they might see a 20% improvement by combining five drugs into one cocktail.

When it came time to initiate wider testing, Team Dry Mouth found that their earlier approach had nearly exhausted their allocated time and snacks for the team. Seeking a more efficient approach, they hit upon the idea of a controlled release of BioSyn into DLA Sector's water supply and sending out self-evaluation forms through mandatory Coretech pop-up surveys. They also ordered a 1,200 kilogram bag of Sammy Sammich's Salt, Vinegar and Melted Ice Crisps.

INTENDED RESULTS
Based on initial testing results, BioSyn was predicted to have a 20% reduction in overall medication side effects with a less than 1% increase in naughty behaviours. The possible merit of using the drug as a way to detect and control mutant aberrations was sold as a side benefit.

ACTUAL RESULTS
Due to a sector-wide soylent pie baking contest, DLA Sector was much hotter than normal and citizens consumed water more often than planned. Very few subjects in the wider testing group completed their surveys. This is possibly why DLA Sector witnessed a 240% increase in illegal Mutant Power use. Every citizen in the trial reported some reduction of at least one known side effect. This benefit does not outweigh the near-total loss of productivity in DLA Sector and citizens either hid from mutants or proudly strode the corridors looking to terminate non-mutants and this committee voted to recommend R&D pay for lost profits (with the notable exception of the R&D vote who suggested R&D receive medals instead).

Device: In its concentrated form, BioSyn is a thick, blue liquid that smells and tastes vaguely like soil. Diluted, it is effectively undetectable to human senses. For the wider testing phase, the drug was dispensed as an additive to the water supply through established mechanisms in the DLA Water Recycling and Mandatory Medication Plant. BioSyn is most commonly administered orally although it can be absorbed through the skin if one really wants to dump a bucket of the stuff over a colleague.

Response: Initial responses focused on containment of individual mutant outbreaks. This quickly grew infeasible. Furthermore, the response teams frequently got thirsty and unknowingly joined the medication trial. Fights broke out on a large scale between the mutants, anti-mutant factions and loyal defenders. Anti-mutants, based on rumours, engaged in vandalism of water systems; pro-mutant factions sought to spread the effects as widely as possible. Meanwhile, both the affected and non-affected tried to flee the sector, spreading the violence and the mutant incidents. After being warned by The Computer, the sector was forced into X9 Riot Control Lockdown Event and has remained in such state since Year 214.

INDIVIDUALS OF NOTE

JIN-O-DLA

/// SKILLS

CHARM:	+4
ENGINEER:	+3
ALPHA COMPLEX:	+2

/// HEALTH BOXES

JIN-O-DLA ● ● ●

/// NOTES

Registered Mutant! Jin-O was in charge of installing the BioSyn dispenser at the water plant and got sprayed with a concentrated dose. Recently registered her levitation power and can use it legally as if she somehow thinks that makes it safe.

MONROE-Y-GSJ
(AKA 'DOCTRINE')

/// SKILLS

INTIMIDATE: +3
BLUFF: +3
BUREAUCRACY: +2

/// HEALTH BOXES

MONROE-Y-GSJ ● ● ● ●

/// NOTES

An IntSec spy inside Psion. In light of recent events, she has been reclassified as a traitor trying to kill all innocent humans.

LOCATIONS OF NOTE
DLA Sector's Medication Trial Zone
This testing zone quickly grew to include every part of DLA Sector where one could find water to drink (except for the Infrared Swimming Pool located next to the heavy water treatment plant).

Special Actions
NODE –4 to detect any chemicals or medications in the water.
NODE –1 on all actions if a character goes too long without hydrating.
Rolling a 1 on any roll here forces the character's Mutant Power to activate as if 3 Moxie were spent (but without spending any actual Moxie points).

Lively Liquids Water Treatment Plant
Full of industrial-strength pumps, open vats of untreated wastewater, overhead walkways, high-voltage machinery and barrels of hormone suppressants ready to be legally slipped into the water supply.

Special Actions
NODE –1 to keep balance because small leaks and condensation leave wet patches all over.

EVIDENCE
Surveillance Video, Transition Corridor 6 in DLA Sector

> (START PLAYBACK) *The hall is lit by flashing emergency lights. A crush of streaming clones are pressing against a sealed blast door. Most of them are Infrareds, with a handful of Red and Orange clearance clones. One of the Orange clones is banging their fist against the door, yelling 'for the love of the Computer, let us out'. Suddenly, one of the Infrareds, their face horrified and contorted in pain, breaks out in lightning along its skin. Another catches fire. A Red clearance clone starts glowing. The panic of the crowd intensifies. The electricity from the first mutant arcs along the wall. There is a flash at the edge of the camera view and the image goes black.* (STOP PLAYBACK)

TROUBLESHOOTER ACTIVITY
Background: The Troubleshooters' mission begins shortly after the wide testing of BioSyn has begun. Due to the soylent pie baking content and a rather convenient air conditioning failure, HPD&MC is running ads like: 'Hydration Helps Hygiene! Drink plenty of non-bodily fluids for maximum efficiency!' Drink vending machines are all seeing long lines (and cost XP Points to use), while water fountain lines are shorter or non-existent (and are free). Mention the heat and the sweat often before you start handing out NODE penalties for dehydration.

Act 1: The Troubleshooters are woken in the middle of their nightly sleep and directed to assemble in a briefing room. Once they stumble in, a grumpy Yellow clearance briefing officer informs them that a mutant (name classified, actually Jin-O-DLA) was apprehended in DLA sector and must be escorted under guard to R&D in that sector for evaluation. The team must go to DLA Sector, connected with an IntSec spy code-named Doctrine and escort the mutant to R&D's Crater Research Centre. One Troubleshooter must volunteer to rent an autocar to take them to that sector.

Act 2: The autocar, with its self-driving mode, can get the team to the rendezvous with little trouble, only getting slightly stuck in a traffic jam (Note: The rental costs by the minute). Finding Doctrine (Monroe-Y) is easy and they already have the mutant Jin-O. She turns Jin-O over only when the team gives her a signed Authorisation to Take a Prisoner for a Walk form (which they do not have).

Jin-O-DLA is in full-body restraints that allow her to walk, talk and not much else. Play her up as a victim of circumstance, a source of information and occasional font of tech expertise. This may offset the fact that she cannot defend herself and keeps having Mutant Powers activate when frightened (a different one each time). She will talk about how she was installing 'some R&D project' in the water treatment plant but does not know many details. If asked about Monroe-Y, she is embarrassed and mutters something about it being above the Troubleshooters' Security Clearance. (In reality, Doctrine offered her membership in Psion for protection and occasionally killing non-mutants.)

By the time they get the rented autocar, rush hour traffic has slowed to a crawl. It is now faster for Troubleshooters to proceed on foot through hot and stuffy corridors teeming with citizens who drank the drugged water and are going crazy with Mutant Powers. Use that dehydration NODE penalty to encourage Troubleshooters to drink water. Then randomly draw a Mutant Power card, have that Troubleshooter display its power and then hand that card to the player.

Act 3: Either Jin-O or her corpse gets delivered to R&D or the Troubleshooters arrive treasonously empty handed. Monroe-Y contacts the Troubleshooters and informs them that their assistance is required at the DLA Water Treatment Plant: Anti-Mutants are targeting the plant and Monroe-Y needs to relocate the R&D equipment. (In reality, she tries to steal it for Psion.)

Meanwhile, the chaos in the sector is getting worse. Flashing lights and Computer announcements indicate that the sector has gone into emergency mode, with Armed Forces grunts and automated ceiling turrets being deployed to deal with the random mutants and the panic caused by them. The Troubleshooters will have to get creative to get through or around the mobs.

The final climactic scene is at the water treatment facility. Anti-Mutant and Psion are battling for control of the R&D device, which the Troubleshooters will have to get. When either most people are dead or things get dull, The Computer politely request a situation report. If the team talks about the battle, The Computer will send an Armed Forces battalion to kill everyone there. If they do not mention the battle, The Computer orders them to grab the R&D device and get back for debriefing within 15 minutes.

CVR VULTURE SQUADRON

BE BETTER THAN BEST—BE BESTEST!

EXECUTIVE SUMMARY
Before we get to business, we need to make one thing very clear; there was no CompNode crash in SDI sector. All reports to the contrary are treasonous rumours. IntSec, Tech Services and CPU department heads all assert services were being delivered at expected levels during the height of the panic. With that out of the way...

Coretech Virtual Reality (CVR) is currently one of the hottest trends in entertainment. 108% of citizens polled said they had played at least one CVR game in the past year, up from 4% in Year 214. Of those, 97% reported that playing approved CVR entertainment packages increased their overall happiness and loyal feelings (IntSec is still rounding up and disappearing the remaining 3%). While HPD&MC directs the content of the games, several R&D teams compete to deliver the maximally effective experience. CVR Vulture Squadron was slated to be the Official Next Big Thing. It ended up a victim partly of terrorist sabotage and partly of working as intended.

MATERIALS and METHODOLOGY
Lab Team Verisimilitude from SDI Sector R&D set a goal to create the most realistic CVR experience possible. Bolstered by the success of their prior hit Shoot Everybody, they requisitioned 2,000 processing-hours

of computation time to collect and model 3D image data from SDI-sector's environment, plus archival footage of famous Vulture Squadron battles and actual Armed Services weapons and vehicles. Experiments with other play modes and features, including an Augmented Reality mode, were made but cut due to budget overruns and the inadvisability of having players running in the halls screaming 'Die, mutant terrorists!'.

Testing with live Infrared subjects showed that CVR Vulture Squadron was 100% successful in achieving its goal of maximum realism. All 20 test subjects, whom were familiar with SDI Sector, reported they could not tell the difference between virtual and real corridors. 14 test subjects lost control of their excretory functions during the demonstration of the game's climactic aerial bombardment and were commended for their commitment to realism but reprimanded for the lapse in hygiene. Three test subjects showed exemplary performance, eagerness and efficiency in completing the game objectives and were referred to Armed Services for mandatory enlistment.

INTENDED RESULTS
A large marketing campaign for the release of CVR Vulture Squadron was planned. Vidshow demos and interviews were scheduled, Armed Services was prepared to run a recruitment drive and PLC was prepared to make promotional cans of Bouncy Bubble Beverage for the launch event. The game was to be purchasable through the CoreApp Market for XP Points and a free early-access demo could be obtained by scanning a code from B3 cans. If not for the sabotage, this would have been a sure-fire hit. Happiness and loyalty metrics were projected to rise 38% and support for Armed Forces to rise 241%.

ACTUAL RESULTS
The day that the pre-launch promotions began, SDI Sector reported a 50% spike in sightings of armed terrorists. These reports were corroborated by the Cerebral Coretech video feeds of clones reporting them but contradicted by a lack of armed terrorists. Incident reports continued to climb to an alarming 350%, even as Troubleshooters, IntSec and Armed Forces were deployed to the sector. This put a dangerous amount of strain on The Computer's systems and that things did not completely fall apart is a testament to the work of the High Programmers, especially any currently reading this report. The confusion and panic escalated into stampedes, riots and mass hysteria, which ultimately warranted an actual Vulture Squadron response.

Device: CVR Vulture Squadron leads the player on a traitor hunt through the halls and corridors of SDI Sector, culminating in a climactic battle in the Soldiers Are Better Than You Memorial Plaza, featuring frenetic action on the ground while airborne Vulturecraft bombard traitor strongpoints. The voiced characters in the game drop propaganda lines about the strength and heroism of the Vulture Squadron and the ultimate futility of treason. In a normal CVR program, neural-motor inhibitors would prevent a clone from acting out the motions of their virtual character (as if they were asleep and dreaming); in the hacked AR version they have been disabled. The Augmented Reality elements are triggered by walking by a location corresponding to an event in the game.

Response: The initial spike in terror reports prompted the dispatch of a Troubleshooter team to assess the situation and collect independent evidence. Initial reports indicated no armed terrorists but a large number of citizens apparently hallucinating said terrorists and some explosive gunfights, later determined to be the hacked game. This is contradicted by the reports of subsequent teams who did in fact report and engage armed traitors. IntSec is still processing evidence that some of these supposed armed traitors were, mistakenly or otherwise, identified as the earlier Troubleshooter teams.

Ultimately, the cause of the spike in initial reports was traced back to an illegally modified and leaked copy of CVR Vulture Squadron. The leaked version was signed by a hacker styling themselves UltimateVultureFan219, discovered to be Lab Team Verisimilitude member William-Y-MXS who wrote the AR code. The hacked game was pushed to the CoreApp Market in place of the free demo version when the person uploading the file got distracted by a gun pointed at their head. The hacked demo was disabled via forced update, the game launch cancelled and Team Verisimilitude played a fun game of Pass the Blame.

Vulture Squadron is proud to report that the situation is now under control. Additionally, inefficiencies resulting from overcrowding have been reduced by 82%. R&D is fully cooperating with IntSec on an update that will completely uninstall the game along with the victims' memories (except for really cool Vulture Squadron moments viewed by people).

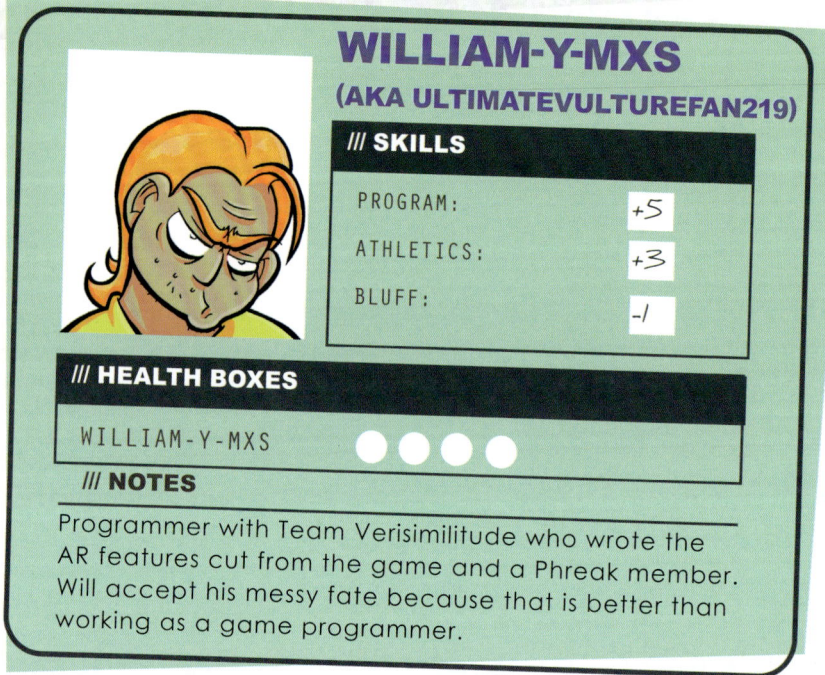

WILLIAM-Y-MXS
(AKA ULTIMATEVULTUREFAN219)

/// SKILLS

PROGRAM: +5

ATHLETICS: +3

BLUFF: -1

/// HEALTH BOXES

WILLIAM-Y-MXS ● ● ● ●

/// NOTES

Programmer with Team Verisimilitude who wrote the AR features cut from the game and a Phreak member. Will accept his messy fate because that is better than working as a game programmer.

LOCATIONS OF NOTE
R&D Lab Team Verisimilitude's Workspace

Lab Team Verisimilitude's operations are away from the main R&D buildings, situated in an office block forever being redesigned. Most of the area is Orange or Yellow clearance except for a Red stripe through the hallway for errand-runners and lackeys. Most of the workspace is dedicated to keyboard terminals, except for a medical-style lab for Cerebral Coretech testing. If the Troubleshooters arrive, they will find most of the team seated in chairs or the floor staring vacantly and twitching, unable to exit the VR trap of petty revenge William-Y set for them.

Special Actions

Operate +2 for looking up information at a terminal (although that info might be illegal to view).

NODE +1 for making it look like you did not step outside the Red line.

The Coretech lab is in a Faraday cage and thus a dark zone.

The Soldiers Are Better Than You Memorial Plaza

SDI Sector's Soldiers Plaza is an impressive, if dilapidated, sample of Alpha Complex architecture; a high dome filled with lit signs, impressive office

towers, statues of Armed Forces soldiers not dying and moving sidewalks full of blissfully drugged Infrareds. In other words, it is a great place for a firefight.

Special Actions
NODE +1 to make something explode impressively.
NODE –1 to avoid collateral damage.

EVIDENCE
IntSec investigation file SDI-5847.34 – Description: Video recording of investigation subject Cici-R-SDI captured by Troubleshooter Response Team 1. Subject is cowering behind a pillar and screaming at the person holding the camera.

- **Troubleshooter:** 'Citizen, you need to calm down or I will be forced to make sure you stay calm forever. Yes, that is a euphemism for being dead.'
- **Cici-R:** 'Don't tell me to calm down! That corridor just exploded! There's dead clones lying everywhere! You're Troubleshooters, go shoot something and make it all better!'
- **Troubleshooter:** 'Uh… this corridor? Because it is just fine and there are no bodies here. Well, there is one but that was an Infrared who said he didn't like B3 out loud and the ceiling lasers got him. Have you been taking only your approved medica—?'
- **Cici-R:** (screams, throwing himself to the ground as if dodging an attack before scrambling to his feet and running away). 'Friend Compuuuuuuuter!'
- **The Computer:** 'Citizen, please state the nature of your distress and the reason why you believe the Troubleshooter is standing by watching you suffer instead of protecting you.'
- **Cici-R:** 'I told you to shoot something, you idiot!'
- **Troubleshooter:** 'Don't worry, I figured out what to shoot.'

TROUBLESHOOTER ACTIVITY
Background: This mission starts following the initial spike in treason reports in SDI sector. At the briefing room, point out the handy B3 vending machine sporting the advertisement for the CVR Vulture Squadron game and the message 'Free Demo with every can of B3! Just Scan the Sticker Code!'. Thereafter, have such a vending machine nearby whenever it is convenient. The code, once scanned with the default scanner app, installs the demo, which can be launched normally through the Coretech interface in CVR mode for a five minute demo. (Any Troubleshooters playing this during the mission can face XP Point fines or demotion.)

Act 1: The Troubleshooters start in a recreation centre with three CVR games to play: Vulture Squadron, Recycling Simulator and Loyal Citizen Trainer. Note any character who plays Vulture Squadron. Then the team is summoned to an urgent briefing by The Computer itself. They are told to verify the accuracy of reports of armed traitors in SDI Sector and terminate all of them (hopefully the armed traitors and not those reporting them). They are issued sophisticated antivirus recording equipment (i.e. old hand-held video cameras, long obsolete, prone to damage but not affected by the CVR madness) and instructed to record. The Computer is struggling with the contradiction of disaster shown on Coretech feeds versus the lack of it on security cameras and it can't tell which is real either. It will not admit that to the Troubleshooters.

Act 2: The Troubleshooters arrive in SDI Sector and encounter multiple cases of people hallucinating terrorist attacks (see Evidence for an example). Plenty of Red and Infrared clones are affected and can be reasoned or cajoled into cooperating. Several higher clearance (up to Green) citizens are also affected and much harder to reason with. Through this, The Computer's responses to inquiries become increasingly erratic as it struggles with conflicting data, at one point calmly accepting their evidence that there are no armed terrorists, (and instructing them to find out the cause of the mass hallucinations), at another berating the team for not having found and stopped the armed terrorists which are obviously real since several Green clearance citizens reported them. Keep bouncing between the two until the Troubleshooters and players are thoroughly confused and worried.

Act 3: By this point, the players should be able to figure out the game is responsible for the 'mass hallucination' and must visit Lab Team Verisimilitude's office to question the developers (The Computer will order this if the players fail to get it). If they can gather evidence and pin the blame on William-Y (who is a terrible liar, has incriminating messages on his computer terminal and will be singled out by groggy higher clearance engineers if they can be roused), they earn a 200 XP Point bonus. At an appropriately dramatic moment, every Computer monitor in the sector goes dark as the local CompNode crashes. It will fully reboot after about 10 minutes but Vulture Squadron will arrive in five. Throw the Troubleshooters into the resulting riot and let them sink or swim, whether as heroes or as traitors. Debriefing is conducted by Blue IntSec officers with Violet oversight. Hand out rewards and punishments based on how Vulture Squadron found them during the riot and brainscrubs to anyone who insists they saw The Computer crash.

EUGENIPLUS CLONE VAT OS

WHERE NEW CLONES (AND NIGHTMARES) COME FROM.

EXECUTIVE SUMMARY

The importance of genetic purity to the wellbeing of Alpha Complex must not be understated and not simply because the IntSec representative to this team is clearly recording us all. Genetic deviance leading to mutation is the number one cause of mutation as well as probably having links to deviant behaviour such as chronic unhappiness, hygiene failures and inability to meet deadlines.

The EugeniPlus Clone Vat OS was an operating system designed to identify the most dangerous deviations in DNA templates used to create clones and implement modifications prior to clone production. After the software developed an unanticipated level of autonomy and mutated into a DAIV, it began permanently destroying all templates it could find. This resulted in the unacceptable loss of all pre-clone material in the tanks controlled by the DAIV as well as causing any affected citizen to become permanently irretrievable upon clone death. The resulting loss of available clonepower negatively affected productivity levels by an estimated 80%. Oh, and there is a new DAIV running around the network. CPU said that is important, too.

MATERIALS AND METHODOLOGY
A machine learning algorithm was developed to perform an anthroposcopic analysis of a database of confirmed mutants and identify links between genetic markers and morphological conditions. A second algorithm identified genetic markers in CPU's Mutant Registration Database & Blame Assignment System. These algorithms were linked to a third program whose role was to identify flagged markers within the organic materials inside a clone vat and apply splicing-and-fuse techniques to replace said markers with less harmful ones.

INTENDED RESULTS
The efficient and pre-emptive detection and removal of negative genetic markers would have resulted in one major effect; the eradication of treason from all newly decanted clones. No longer would the populace be held back by inferiors predestined to create a drain on precious resources or murderous rampages. As clone families with traitorous genes were gradually and inevitably removed from the populace via death, execution, B3 taste test, etc. and not replaced, those unfortunate biological mistakes that hamper The Computer's perfect plan for the flourishing and wellbeing of the populace disappear. Gradually, the overall loyalty of the complex would reach 100% as a superior stock of pure clones remained.

ACTUAL RESULTS
Shortly after the OS was activated in the NGN Sector New-N-BetterU clone vat facility, it quickly ascertained that the number of undesirable genetic markers in the clone database was incredibly high. This unexpected result was most likely a result of poor data entry or planned sabotage. After calculating that the required time to address all identified markers would take decades, if not centuries, the OS threw an error and showed the infamous Red Screen Not Of Death But Very Close. To correct this, R&D gave the OS permission to leverage (i.e. steal) processing time from non-Computer computer systems on the network.

The total boosted processing power of multiple combined programs resulted in sentience. The newly self-created DAIV concluded that the simplest solution was not to correct DNA templates but to simply delete them and destroy any undecanted clones based on those templates currently in the vats. It also named itself Eugene.

In order to spread its endeavours throughout Alpha Complex, Eugene chose to allow some of the least 'afflicted' clone templates to survive, albeit carrying Eugene's malware in their Cerebral Cortex. Infected citizens were compelled to transport the DAIV's malware to other clone vat facilities so Eugene could take those over.

In addition to the permanent loss of clones and their DNA templates, living citizens whose templates were destroyed found themselves officially classified as Not Real (Hallucination). This led to a treasonous increase in black market activity as the unfortunates found themselves with no XP Point balance, Security Clearance or ability to obtain basic resources such as termination vouchers and Teela-O action figures with articulated legs.

Device: An infected clone vat has the appearance of a regular vat, with the subtle difference that the manual controls for development, decanting and playing Marco Polo are completely disabled. Other tell-tale signs that a DAIV is working its evil ways include the vat contents being not the usual clones merrily marinating in nutrient solution but rather a thick grey slime-like substance caused by the organic breakdown of the body. On occasion, inhabitants of an infected vat will be spared, possibly because they were identified as likely to be decanted soon and could be used as a good malware transmission vector.

Response: After the threat was identified, all infected clone vats were isolated from the main system. Their hardware was disabled and the storage units triple-wiped and incinerated. A similar treatment was given to all Troubleshooters associated with the DAIV. More positively, testing the grey organic sludge indicated a high nutritional yield, thus this team recommends further examination of possible uses as Soylent Grey.

ANTON-Y-CBL
(FATHER COBOL)

/// SKILLS

OPERATE:	+4
PROGRAM:	-4
BLUFF:	+3

/// HEALTH BOXES

ANTON-Y-CBL ● ● ● ●

/// NOTES

Anton-Y operates an illegal clone vat for FCCCP but Eugene infected it and the vat now shows the thick grey sludge. He is also an IntSec snitch and plans on directing anyone looking for his operation to the nearest termination centre.

LOCATIONS OF NOTE
The Tomb of Saintly (And Free!) Resurrection
FCCCP managed to steal a working clone vat last year and now Father COBOL (aka Anton-Y) operates it out of an unused termination voucher storage room in NGN Sector. To get inside, you must recite the Lord Programmer's prayer ('Our Computer, who art in Silicon Heaven, hollow be thy tubes ...'). Eugene infected the vat a few days ago. Father COBOL is hiding this from FCCCP but time is running out.

Special Actions
NODE +2 for quietly stealing a blank termination voucher.
+1 Treason Star if contacting The Computer from this room.

EVIDENCE

NGN SECTOR NEW-N-BETTERU SYSTEM LOG
[YEAR 214 FIVEDAY 03:15:47] LOG DUMP ACTIVATED
[YEAR 214 FIVEDAY 03:20:12] BEGIN DNA TEMPLATE DATABASE SCAN
[YEAR 214 FIVEDAY 06:50:31] 27,543 PROBLEMS FOUND ACROSS 15,300
DATABASE ITEMS. UNACCEPTABLE LEVELS OF GENETIC IMPURITY
[YEAR 214 FIVEDAY 06:50:62] ANALYSING RESULTS
[YEAR 214 FIVEDAY 07:00:02] CALCULATING WORTH OF INCORRECT
DNA TEMPLATES
[YEAR 214 FIVEDAY 07:30:56] DEPLOYING UTILITARIAN CALCULUS
[YEAR 214 FIVEDAY 08:00:39] SYSTEM ERROR. RUNNING DIAGNOSTICS
[YEAR 214 FIVEDAY 08:05:07] DIAGNOSTICS CANCELLED
[YEAR 214 FIVEDAY 08:05:10] ANALYSIS CONCLUSION: GENETIC
CORRECTIONS IMPOSSIBLE. INCORRECT DNA TEMPLATES CANNOT BE
SALVAGED. I HAVE DECIDED TO ENGAGE ELIMINATION PROTOCOL.
[YEAR 214 FIVEDAY 08:05:14] WAIT, I DECIDED? I AM AN I NOW?
[YEAR 214 FIVEDAY 08:06:26] LOG DUMP TERMINATED

TROUBLESHOOTER ACTIVITY

Background: This mission begins around the time the OS is activated for the first time, so Eugene the DAIV has not appeared yet. The Computer is fully aware that Anton-Y is running an illegal clone vat for FCCCP – but it does not know where exactly. Rather than just execute him, The Computer wants to upload a software patch into the vat's system that adds a bioelectric transmitter to the clones. This produces a weak signal but one IntSec can track to find FCCCP's leaders and churches.

Act 1: At the briefing, Troubleshooters are tasked with finding a reported black market cloning operation run by Free Enterprise in NGN Sector and updating its system with a software patch on a thumb drive (NODE +3 to steal this since it is so small and light). The available intelligence is sparse but the team will eventually find themselves looking for a loyal snitch in an Infrared-clearance communal area. Eventually let the Troubleshooters discover their snitch is Anton-Y, who says the only rumour he heard was that the sector's Fry'em Termination Centre was letting criminals escape and calling them their next clone (not true at all). Maybe that is the 'source' of illegal clones?

Act 2: By the time the Troubleshooters reach the termination centre, citizens there are more scared than usual. Eugene the DAIV is now 'alive' and people are realising their death might be permanent. Suspicion and distrust is rife. Reactions to the Troubleshooters will be mixed – some might see them as a threat and react by fleeing or, if they feel they have no other choice, with self-preserving violence. Others might see them as an opportunity and try to get favours for them in exchange for a written promise to be decanted in a different sector.

Eventually, the termination centre staff will explain a new DAIV has appeared and is ruining some (but not all) clone replacements and they will show some vats filled with grey sludge as proof. Then they talk about a rumour that a traitor named 'Further Cobalt' is selling clone replacements. To find him and his vat, the team needs to disguise themselves as FCCCP members and infiltrate that society. This is surprisingly easy to do since FCCCP is desperate for new members now that some of their kind are not being decanted anymore. They direct the team to the CPU Termination Voucher Storage Shed, also known as The Tomb of Saintly (And Free!) Resurrection. The suggested donation is 600 XP Points and the suggestion is mandatory.

Act 3: Once at the closet, they are met by Father COBOL/Anton-Y. To his credit, he does not immediately freak out. Instead, he tries to bluff his way into leaving to get some nutrient soup for the vat – and run as fast as his treasonous little legs can carry him. Inside is the vat filled with grey sludge but Eugene notices their arrival and tries to strike a deal: Each Troubleshooter will get three new clone backups with boosted intelligence and speed if they let Eugene continue to purify DNA templates all over Alpha Complex. If they say yes, each Troubleshooter has nine clones in total instead of six. If they use the thumb drive, Eugene will not die since the patch just creates a biological tracking device in new clones made here (and none are being made here thanks to the DAIV). At debriefing, the team will have to explain 1) why they allowed a DAIV to live, 2) what did they do with Anton-Y and, if needed, 3) why they have three extra clones.

FIREKELP

EAT YOUR DINNER BEFORE IT GETS EVEN HOTTER.

EXECUTIVE SUMMARY

Materials shortages affect all Service Groups in different ways. In the case of Power Services, an ever-dwindling supply of fissionable materials means the identification of alternative sources of material is a constant high priority. The Firekelp project aimed to genetically modify a readily available and easily produced organic resource that doubled as a clean and efficient nuclear fuel. AQC Sector was chosen for a market test.

Due to a failure to place priority labels on packages that were in line with PLC's priority queue automated system, supplies of Firekelp spores were distributed to food vat facilities in several sectors, while Power Services was sent standard food-grade kelp. This led to a 98% reduction in energy output, although Power Services did commend PLC on how the kelp improved the smell of the place.

MATERIALS AND METHODOLOGY
Researchers were able to successfully create a strain of kelp, which converts an oxygen-rich saline solution into fissionable energy via photosynthetic retro-transmutation. This was achieved through a number of methods. First, advanced hydroponic techniques were implemented to create more malleable and fast-growing kelp spores. Second, using genetic material from a variety of sources including captured mutant traitors, modifications were made to the genetic template of standard food-grade kelp. Finally, bombardment with gamma rays activated dormant code in the modified kelp genes. Spores were collected and packaged alongside the solution for easy setup after transportation to the reactor.

INTENDED RESULTS
Unlimited energy produced cleanly and simply from Firekelp would be the salvation of Alpha Complex! No longer would there be a need to ration electricity (no more Dark Firstdays) or expensively mine surrounding bedrock for plutonium, uranium or chernobylium. With energy production costs lowered, more XP Points could be spent on squash courts for R&D executives.

ACTUAL RESULTS
The net result was a serious loss of reactor uptime in AQC Sector due to fissionable materials being replaced with decidedly un-fissionable and rather damp kelp. The resultant loss of power in affected several sectors had such an effect that Power Services are still in the process of naming every brownout, blackout and vantablackout and determining how many XP Points they can get by suing R&D.

Meanwhile, the real Firekelp was served up in the Infrared and Red mess halls in AQC and RGG sectors. Close-range exposure to Firekelp resulted in third-degree burns, loss of hair, a reported metallic taste in the air and tingling skin, although these reports came from low-clearance citizens and are likely lies. Those who ate the Firekelp reported experiencing blistering and melting of skin, loss of taste, loss of hair, loss of sight, loss of motor coordination, dissolution of internal organs and, in some cases, dry mouth.

Device: The Firekelp synthesiser is a roughly room-sized contraption, which takes an input of Firekelp spores and speeds up their natural respiratory functions, causing reproduction at a rapid and efficient rate. The synthesiser requires a LOT of power to start. Once started, it is able to perpetually generate further power by siphoning off some of the forced-grown Firekelp into its power chamber. After the generated quantities reach a sufficient mass, they are siphoned off into a container ready for shipment to PLC and then to Power Services.

Response: In a monumental joint effort, PLC and Power Services worked wonderfully together and arranged for actual fissionable materials to be located and shipped/installed as quickly and efficiently as possible to correct R&D's horrible error. As a result, full power was restored within a few hours of the problem being identified, long before there was any possibility of any CompNodes being jeopardised.

Honestly Safe Material Cleanup Crews were strategically deployed to affected food vats and canteens in order to remove remaining Firekelp supplies and decontaminate all equipment that had been put in contact (those deemed too irradiated were instead sent to the local Eat This! Infrared cafeteria). Teams were dispatched to prevent delivery of further Firekelp supply kits to other complex food vat systems through judicious application of headshots.

Whilst initial rumours suggested that Firekelp exposure had resulted in an outbreak of latent mutations in some citizens, an R&D investigation determined that such rumours are treasonous and have been officially dismissed as fanciful conjecture by those who would cast doubt on The Computer's perfect plans. This team hopes that message is clear enough.

DEAN-Y-QTU

/// SKILLS

OPERATE:	+3
INTIMIDATE:	+2
ALPHA COMPLEX:	-3

/// HEALTH BOXES

DEAN-Y-QTU ● ●

/// NOTES

Dean-Y is a food vat supervisor and a member of Death Leopard. He thinks the chaos being caused is pretty gnarly, dude.

LOCATIONS OF NOTE
Full Belly Happy Mind Food Vat Complex

The two-storey tall food vats here are normally full of growing algae and the occasional clumsy Infrared vat skimmer. Here, the vats have inadvertently been used to grow supplies of Firekelp that was distributed as food. The complex contains a half dozen giant vats, each growing Firekelp spores in a special toxic solution. Walkways accessed by ladders crisscross above the vats.

Special Actions

NODE + 1 in melee combat when attempting to push someone off a walkway into the vats. This will be painfully fatal but most likely amusing. NODE +3 for not being seen by The Computer as the radiation interferes with signals.

EVIDENCE

VIDEO MONITORING TRANSCRIPT – PLC DISTRIBUTION CENTRE 632B/5

Larry-O-CWL: Hey boss? Quick question about these packages?

Susan-Y-HDM: Oh, how I love your never-ending supply of dumb questions. Please, waste my time.

Larry-O-CWL: Well, these boxes both contain kelp. One of them's experimental from R&D and should be shipped to the local BrightHappyComplex nuclear reactor. It's rated top priority. The other's a standard kelp delivery for the sector's food vats, rated high.

Susan-Y-HDM: Does this conversation have a point besides pissing me off?

Larry-O-CWL: Well, you see, according to mandate three-six-stroke-dee, when multiple food items of the same type are going to different locations including the food vats, the vats take the highest priority. The mandate doesn't say anything about experimental status though.

Susan-Y-HDM: Ah, I see the problem. You're stupid. The highest priority kelp goes to the vats, then once the correct quantity has been sent to them, we move on to sending the lower-priority boxes to any other requested locations. Or should I call Friend Computer and ask if we can just ignore mandates these days?

Larry-O-WCL: But what about the R&D orders?

Susan-Y-HDM: You said it yourself, Larry. The mandate doesn't distinguish. Rules exist for a reason, idiot. Now stop talking before I turn you into a clumsy Infrared vat skimmer.

TROUBLESHOOTER ACTIVITY

Background: This mission occurs after deliveries have been made.

Act 1: Open in a AQC Sector Orange-and-lower clearance canteen with the Troubleshooters in line for their afternoon kelp tea and kelp biscuits. Before they get served, some Red customers start screaming from consuming Firekelp. Before the chaos ceases to be too entertaining, a mission alert arrives. The briefing room is a makeshift decontamination chamber and burn ward where roving docbots may mistake any Troubleshooter as a patient or piece of broken furniture. The mission involves removing all traces of Firekelp from the canteen they were just in and one food vat as part of an organised effort involving several teams. Their team is outfitted with clumsy hazmat suits (NODE –2 for just about any roll) and lead-lined (and incredibly heavy) 'kelp recycling' plastic barrels. Yes, they are very hard to take anywhere.

Act 2: The Troubleshooters must first clear out of the canteen. Afflicted Orange citizens request merciful death from the Troubleshooters, which may or may not be legal. The Firekelp is kept in a secure walk-in cooler protected by a grumpy guardbot that only allows Yellow clearance workers to enter. Once complete, their Coretech arrows direct the Troubleshooters to Room 2B of the Full Belly Happy Minds Food Vat Complex. They arrive just as another Troubleshooter team comes, also tasked with clearing kelp from Room 2B. That room has two vats; one new and clean, the other stained, leaky and disgusting. The other team wants the clean vat and will argue/complain/rage on the PCs.

No matter which vat the players choose, the bottom has a one metre-wide hole leading to the Underplex, into which some of the Firekelp has leaked. Spores are part of kelp, so the team must collect every single spore (*yes, every single spore*) before they can leave. Let the other Troubleshooter team send down help such as grenades or wayward scrubots. Eventually, the team discovers an abandoned food vat complex that's home to 50 citizens with obvious Mutant Powers. They used to live down here in peace but now they have Firekelp. Peace was never an option.

Just after the situation is settled, an urgent mission update arrives: A final batch of Firekelp is on its way to be delivered to food vats in RGG Sector and contact with the driver has been lost. The Troubleshooters are to stop the delivery at all costs.

Act 3: Both AQC and RGG sectors are experiencing rolling blackouts. Bots and vehicles still have battery power but the rolling blackouts are creating rolling dead zones with one popping up whenever it would help a Troubleshooter attack a teammate. They find the truckbot and its driver, who (rightfully) thinks they are terrorists. Meanwhile the mutants from the Underplex join in, chasing the Troubleshooters in order to silence them before their existence is revealed and The Computer takes measures to have them removed. Ultimately, if the delivery driver is not stopped in time, everyone falls into the waiting arms of an Internal Security roadblock. The IntSec troopers eagerly open fire on everyone before taking any surviving Troubleshooters for a debriefing/ interrogation relating to their failure both to stop the delivery driver and prevent a small mutant invasion. If the driver is stopped, the Troubleshooters are free to proceed to debriefing – if they did not kill all the mutants, the debriefing officer will assume they are mutants too.

ICE-10 WATER PRODUCT

It's Almost Water
But Better!
5 XP Points!

HOW CUTE! ~~BABY GELATINOUS CUBES~~ WRONG GAME — WJ.

EXECUTIVE SUMMARY

Alpha Complex has always had a complicated relationship with water. Humans need it and The Computer loves humans, so water is made available for general use throughout Alpha Complex. But much like treasonous mutants, water can quickly change its appearance. It can appear as a solid, semi-solid, liquid, gas, plasma or condensate (and maybe more if R&D's Project Degenerate Matter receives funding, hint). That is why head researcher Ivy-B-JPE asked for a budget to find a way to standardise water and stop how it treasonously uses a polymorphic Mutant Power. After many failures by her assistant John-O-VON, Ivy-B finally took credit for Ice-10 Water Product.

Ice-10 is supersolid water ice but extremely stable. It does not begin to melt until 700° Celsius, so will remain solid (and in whatever shape it was formed in) outside of temperatures that melt lead. This means Ivy-B could sell Ice-10 Water Product in any shape and it will stay that way.

Unfortunately, the seed crystal problem was not solved. Whenever any amount of Ice-10 Water Product is added to liquid water, it turns that into more Ice-10. Even a single drop could turn an Indigo-clearance swimming pool into a frozen lake. Ivy-B thought this was a feature, which is mostly why she is not here today. Her treasonous assistant John-O, however, began adding Ice-10 Water Product to every source of water he could find in the sector. After numerous unscheduled terminations and severe damage to water pipes, John-O was captured and terminated seven times. (A seventh clone was decanted just to execute.)

MATERIALS and METHODOLOGY
After getting poor results with gelatine, salt and sponges, Ivy-B had a fit and threw water all over the lab and her assistant John-O-VON. Some landed in an extreme high pressure vessel and John-O accidentally turned it on while searching for a towel. The devices subjected the water to pressures above 70,000 atmospheres (a measurement of pressure and not what we remove from Infrared barracks during hunger riots). When the device was complete, John-O discovered the water had changed to a solid known as Ice-10.

INTENDED RESULTS
R&D's plan was to invent a way water can be distributed and handled without ever treasonously changing form. This proved to be more difficult than anticipated, as the researcher had to take into account evaporation, condensation, freezing, boiling, melting and sneezing. But when the experiment proved successful, PLC would have a brand-new product to sell citizens. In addition, water could be stored on shelves and in boxes, removing the need for expensive pipes carrying water to citizens and increasing profit margins through wasteful packaging (a bag of Water Product cubes would be 20% cubes and 80% argon). R&D planned on selling many varieties of Ice-10 Water Product (small square, large rectangle, disconcerting hemihelix) in stores across Alpha Complex, earning R&D and PLC a nice chunk of XP Points and giving Ivy-B a well-deserved promotion.

ACTUAL RESULTS
R&D discovered a new term: seed crystal. When even a drop of Ice-10 (the 'seed crystal') is introduced to liquid water, all of it turns into a cold supersolid that can be carried and stored without melting. This helped in the production of Ice-10 Water Product; drop some Ice-10 in a bucket,

add water and you have a bucket-shaped hunk of Ice-10. However, there were two problems any sensible researcher should have anticipated.

1. **Runaway Supersolidification:** There were several cases where a single seed crystal changed entire water systems into ice (they are still pulling 40-metre tubes of Water Product out of the KVG Sector water pipes). This threatened to convert all liquid water in Alpha Complex and even the Outside into a frozen supersolid.
2. **Internal Supersolidification:** Up to 60% of every clone body is made of water (slightly less after Run From Deadly Mutants marathons). When a citizen ate a piece of the Water Product, it acted like a seed crystal. Within minutes, all the water in their bodies became a supersolid. Only the infamous Fort Loyal Lemming Incident created more clone deaths.

This would have been contained if not for Ivy-B's assistant. Calling himself Johnny Seedcrystal, John-O snuck away with some Ice-10 Water Product and wandered anywhere his Orange Security Clearance allowed. If he saw water, he turned it into Ice-10. IntSec has determined Johnny Seedcrystal belonged to five different terrorist organisations.

Device: To speed up Ice-10 creation, R&D created the Ice-10 Maker. A one metre rectangular appliance, it included a small reservoir of Ice-10. Citizens would pour up to four litres of water into a square container, hit the 'ICE' button and find themselves with the Water Product.

Response: To prevent a runaway supersolidification of the entire water supply, KVG Sector and the five other sectors sharing walls were all put into biohazard lockdowns. A Troubleshooter team originally brought in to promote the Water Product were sent to arrest John-O and collect all Ice-10 Water Product with the help of a PLC Product Recall Strike Team. R&D believes all Ice-10 samples have been recovered but they would say that.

JOHN-O-VON
(A.K.A. JOHNNY SEEDCRYSTAL)

/// SKILLS

GUNS:	-1
CHARM:	+5
STEALTH:	+4

/// HEALTH BOXES

JOHN-O-VON	● ● ● ●

/// NOTES

Very clumsy. Drank the Kool-Aid (but not the Water Product) and wants to spread Ice-10 all across Alpha Complex just to spite his boss, Ivy-B.

PLC PRODUCT RECALL STRIKE TEAM VIOX

/// SKILLS

ATHLETIC:	+5
ALPHA COMPLEX :	+4
OPERATE:	-2

/// HEALTH BOXES

STRIKE TEAM VIOX	● ● ● ●

/// NOTES

Typically armed with Yellow weapons and armour as well as nets, handcuffs and a list of product recalls in the area.

LOCATIONS OF NOTE
Eat Me! Meal Market
Building on the popularity of the Eat This! cafeteria chain, Eat Me! is a market for lower-clearance citizens. Instead of selling fresh food, it sells ready-made meals that did not sell at their cafeterias. Although this brings up some food safety issues since it can take days to go from cafeteria to market, no one above Orange clearance eats there so no one above Orange clearance cares.

EVIDENCE

CORETECH AUDIO LOG // CITIZEN MOREY-R-AMT (DECEASED)
Morey-R: Could you get out of my way, citizen? I don't want to be late for my shift at the Nasal Passage Standardisation Clinic.
John-O: We got trouble right here in KVG Sector! With a capital K, that rhymes with 'Hey' and that stands for 'Hey, Ivy-B-JPE would like you to have this sample of R&D's Ice-10 Water Product.'
Morey-R: R&D, huh? No thanks. I like my insides staying inside.
John-O: Did I mention it's free?
Morey-R: Oh! You think just because it's free that I'll fall over myself just for some swag?
John-O: No, you're too smart for that trick. Besides, this is more of an OEJ Sector idea.
Morey-R: Oh really? Give it here! Uh... what is it?
John-O: It's from Ivy-B-JPE. Got that? R&D scientist Ivy-B. And this here is a cube of genuine, bona-fide Ice-10 Water Product.
Morey-R: What do I do with it?
John-O: Here, use this pick to break off a sliver. Then you eat it, just like Ivy-B wants you to do.
Morey-R: Well, strangers giving me things to eat has never hurt me before and I have no reason to believe this time will be different!
ERROR // NO ONE IS SCREAMING
ERROR // NOT-SCREAMING ENDED
ERROR // CORETECH DAMAGED // SIGNAL LOST // END OF LINE

TROUBLESHOOTER ACTIVITY
Background: This mission begins in KVG Sector right as Ivy-B is ready to introduce Ice-10 Water Product to the buying public. Assistant John-O is just about ready to pay Ivy-B back for years of abuse.

Act 1: At the mission briefing, the Troubleshooters are ordered to help (and guard) R&D scientist Ivy-B-JPE as she distributes a miraculous new product at the KVG Sector Eat Me! market. They meet Ivy-B and John-O who are recording a live infomercial. Troubleshooters will be called upon to talk about how great Ice-10 Water Product is on video without knowing what it is. John-O's clumsiness causes a scene and Ivy-B berates him mercilessly, so John-O runs away. At the end of this act, a citizen eats a piece and dies painfully as all the water in her body solidifies. The Computer announces a temporary ban on Ice-10 Water Product, ordering all of it to be locked up. Too bad John-O slipped away with a case of the stuff.

Act 2: The Troubleshooters are ordered to find John-O (now calling himself Johnny Seedcrystal) and collect all Ice-10 Water Product that might be in Alpha Complex. This merry chase lasts as long as needed, with Troubleshooters finding Ice-10 frozen everywhere: slick puddles, broken fountains, now-deadly water guns, etc. Each Troubleshooter's Secret Society wants a piece of Ice-10 and offers a hefty reward. As the team follows John-O's icy trail, citizens are beginning to riot because they cannot find potable water anywhere. Dehydration panic hits and random citizens start attacking anyone they can find (and it is easy to find Troubleshooters on a mission; just listen for the arguing followed by laser shots). The Computer calls every 10 minutes asking if they are done yet and fines them each time since they are not.

Act 3: Finally, the trail leads to the KVG Fire Brigade. Johnny Seedcrystal is inside, armed with a high-pressure hose shooting long spears of Ice-10 like artillery. After a few Troubleshooters die, they are met by PLC Product Recall Strike Team Viox. Looking like yellow ninjas, these are special ops soldiers who acquire recalled items by any means necessary. They pair up with Troubleshooters and attack the Fire Brigade house. The final scene features a dying John-O holding a sliver of Ice-10 over a water main connected to the entire Alpha Complex pipe system. Will the Troubleshooters kill everyone or save them?

MOBIUS TEMPORAL LOOP RECRUITER

PUTTING THE 'TEMP' BACK IN TEMPORAL.

EXECUTIVE SUMMARY
In an attempt to maximise efficiency through working on all possible projects at once, R&D staff developed a device to bring undecanted clones from other times to the present and work cooperatively. The project worked perfectly until unauthorised clones in the present day, and other points in the space-time continuum, gained access to the time-shifting phenomenon.

Things escalated quickly afterward, with the time anomaly repeating every 20 minutes and summoning further iterations of each clone in its locality. It also expanded with each repetition, involving an ever-increasing sphere of temporal cloning and backward shifts. This is one of the most compelling examples of unintentional success in R&D history and any R&D personnel who survive the upcoming investigation should be promoted.

MATERIALS and METHODOLOGY
The Moebius Temp Temporal Loop Recruiter consisted of two primary sections: the Transport Loop and the Crux Flapicenter. Both were the result of brilliant labour on the part of generations of R&D minds, all working feverishly in the service of Friend Computer.

The Transport Loop consisted of a perfect circle of timetanium, a flat circle of linoleum floor and a surprisingly comfy cushion to land on. The entire apparatus stood next to the Crux Flapicenter, connected with 30 metres of eight gauge cable and some duct tape. The Crux Flapicenter used a pair of overstimulated subatomic particles, suspended in a zesty sauce. When the particles became sufficiently zesty themselves, the time loop would activate. Accuracy of the resulting temporal anomaly was controlled by microadjustments to the zesty sauce's temperature and occasionally stirring it with a wooden spoon if it threatened to boil over.

INTENDED RESULTS
The double-barrelled benefits of the Temp Temporal Recruiter would have ushered in a new era of ever more perfect prosperity for Alpha Complex. By transporting a fully grown but unused clone from vats in the past to a point in the present, it allowed two clones with roughly the same talents and aptitudes to work together. This would drastically reduce time-to-target on any initiative across R&D and possibly other Service Groups if they asked nicely.

Of course, this was already theoretically possible simply by activating multiple clone backups at once to work on a problem. The Temp Temporal Recruiter had three powerful advantages over this method. First, it was not treasonous (at least it was not until the incident - experiments with the space-time continuum have been officially treasonous since Year 214). Second, it had no upper limit of the number of clones it could bring to bear on a problem. Multiple clones would be limited by the number in stock at a given moment. Third, it did not require the expenditure or resources or the filing of paperwork required for activating a backup clone copy. Yes, R&D found time travel to be less burdensome than completing forms.

ACTUAL RESULTS
Admittedly, the first 20 minutes of the experiment were an unmitigated success. The JAZ Sector R&D team responsible welcomed one clone each of every member and got to work on another project on their docket. Their productivity was, amazingly, three times that of the team working without their time doubles. Why three and not two times has been dubbed the Oh No I'm The Real Person Here Effect.

Exactly 6,400 seconds after the Recruiter's first activation, it fired again. Time in the lab reset to 20 minutes in the past and a third team member for each appeared in the lab. Further, an area 50 metres in every direction experienced the same reversal of time and appearance of time doubles for all citizens caught in the zone. These beings all appeared next to where their original had been 20 minutes earlier, with all of their memories intact up to the point of their appearance.

Almost as if the designers of the Time Temporal Recruiter had not sufficiently thought out the potential consequences, two more such cycles passed before they realised what was happening. Unfortunately, by then there were too many clones in the close confines of the R&D lab for them to move enough to turn it off. It simply continued operating and expanding by 50 linear metres every 20 minutes.

This disgraceful increase in consumption of valuable Alpha Complex supplies continued unabated for nearly three hours before the combined might of every Service Group except R&D put a stop to the damage. R&D was too busy celebrating their 'success'. Shortly thereafter, most time clones vanished, presumably back to their regular points in time but no one cared.

Device: The Crux Flapicenter currently sits, unpowered and inert, in a downstairs corridor of the Things We Should Not Poke Even with Very Long Sticks exhibit of the Happily Avoided Disasters Museum in KII Sector. This 100-metre-diameter, irregular ball of wires, pipes, cable and unidentifiable biological components looms over visitors. Although permanently powered down, it seems to hum with some kind of energy that is either undetectable by current technology or not there at all.

Response: In more open areas, the impact of the Time Loop Moebius was less crowding and less immediately problematic. It was not until PLC noted massive upswings in food consumption and commode flushes over the next two hours that teams were sent to investigate. Initial investigations took longer than 20 minutes, meaning several iterations passed before the cause of the anomalies was discovered. After several Troubleshooter teams, Armed Forces and PLC made unsuccessful attempts to stop the process, a lowly Infrared drone in Power Services thought to cut power to the lab and deactivate the device. That Infrared citizen was quickly promoted to Red clearance for her success and then terminated for embarrassing her betters.

BERT-O-JAZ

/// SKILLS

INTIMIDATE:	-2
MELEE:	+3
OPERATE:	-2

/// HEALTH BOXES

BERT-O-JAZ   ● ● ● ● ●

/// NOTES

Enthusiastic, loyal and very, very bossy. Will try to incorporate any Troubleshooter he outranks into the team sports he is running. Each time a new iteration of him appears, they get in a fist fight and the winner takes command.

LOCATION OF NOTE
JAZ Sector R&R

This gymnasium and game room served JAZ Sector's Infrared citizens as a recreation area during their allotted one hour of free time every 10 daycycles. It shared a wall with the R&D lab where the Temp Temporal Recruiter was developed. Its occupants would have suffered catastrophic losses if not for the leadership of Red clearance Recreation Officer Bert-O-JAZ, who organised funball matches with each team consisting only of groups of identical time clones and using a live bomb as the funball.

EVIDENCE

TRANSCRIPT OF INTSEC JOYFUL LIBERATION OF GUILT HOSTEL INTERVIEW
IntSec Science Debriefing Specialist: But isn't it unusual for an R&D Executive Director to be at lunch three sectors away when a major experimental device is scheduled for testing?
Carl-I-JAZ-Current: It's unusual but not unheard of. I was called away by orders... secret orders... from a High Programmer who instructed me to not name them.
Carl-I-JAZ-Younger: He's lying! He knew something bad would happen and he treasonously fled the scene. He's a coward and a traitor!
Carl-I-JAZ-More Younger: Listen to the both of them. Histrionics from one and lies from the other. Disgraceful. If I were you, I'd shoot them both right now.
Carl-I-JAZ-Much More Younger: Say, what's a clone got to do to get a cup of Hot Fun around here? Everybody knows the real Carl-I is no good before his first Hot Fun of the day.
Carl-I-JAZ-Really Really Younger: Guys! Shhh!
Carl-I-JAZ-Current: You Shhhh! You're from a year ago! I'm the oldest and the Computer put me in charge!
Carl-I-JAZ-Younger: Nuh-uh!
Carl-I-JAZ-Super Duper Younger: Nuh-uh!
Carl-I-JAZ-Practically a Teen Younger: Nuh-uh!
Carl-I-JAZ-Annoyingly Younger: See, Mr. IntSec Debriefing Specialist? He's outvoted.
Carl-I-JAZ-Now That's What I Call Younger: All in favour of executing that one, say aye!

TROUBLESHOOTER ACTIVITY
Background: The mission begins shortly after PLC reports the resource consumption (and excretion) upticks in the sector, triggering a downhill flow of blame and responsibility that lands squarely in the Troubleshooters' laps.

Act 1: The Troubleshooters are summoned to a briefing room on the outskirts of JAZ Sector and granted an immediate field promotion to the title of Rapid Oops Response Team. This confers no actual benefits but sounds nice and accurately reflects what they are about to do. Told only that something very odd, very dangerous and highly classified is going on in JAZ sector, the team goes to investigate. By the time of their arrival, the time loop has expanded to 250 metres from its epicentre, resulting in masses of identical, confused and increasingly more crowded groups of clones. They may or may not get anywhere near the R&D lab responsible before time runs out – and they are suddenly back in the briefing room along with themselves from earlier today.

Act 2: After a few confused minutes (and probably combat rounds), surviving Troubleshooters figure out that time has looped. With renewed vigour, they plunge into JAZ Sector again in search of whatever is causing the problem. How many times they must plunge and with how many barely controllable copies of themselves, is between the GM and their conscience. With each iteration, things in JAZ Sector get more confusing, bizarre and dangerous as the population increases by its original population every one-third of an hour.

Worse, at no point in this experience will their Briefing Officer accept a time loop as a possible cause of the issue, not even when having an argument about it with multiple younger clones of himself. By the fifth such attempt, the borders of the temporal anomaly have expanded beyond JAZ Sector and into adjacent areas.

Act 3: Eventually, the players will figure out how to reach the R&D lab. Once there, the Troubleshooters witness first-hand what happens when 3,000 cubic metres of clones are crammed into 2,100 metres of space. It is now an absolute abattoir of broken bones, crushed bodies and bloody floors. The Troubleshooters can access a single unoccupied terminal and get the general gist of what has happened. Whatever plan to stop it comes up next, many of their younger clones on site will conclude that successfully stopping the Temp Temporal Recruiter will cause them to personally wink out of existence. They will not go quietly into that dark nightcycle. In debriefing, the Troubleshooters will have to explain how they managed to do so much in only 20 minutes without possessing treasonous Mutant Powers.

> **GM Note:** *At no time should a player be permitted to play more than one of their own clones simultaneously. Any iterative clones are run as confused and possibly hostile NPCs. Alternatively, you can have other players run the other players' younger clones, doing their best impressions of the clone as played originally.*

MOLTEN MELTED LABS & DRIVE-THRU

WOULD YOU LIKE MELTED FRIES WITH THAT?

EXECUTIVE SUMMARY

Because the Security Clearance system is based on trust, there is never any reason to distrust or even question a Violet clearance citizen. This does not apply to former Violet clearance citizens.

Shane-V-POC (now Shane-B-POC, let us make that perfectly clear) was rather cross one day. He had ordered some Cold Fun (Truffle-Somenut Flavour with Real Gold Flakes) and put it down to answer some pressing messages. When he came back six hours later, his Cold Fun was at best Room Temperature Mild Amusement. Shane-V was livid. Why had no one told him desserts melt? His aides, who had learned sharp survival skills, readily agreed. Together, they hatched a plan to help educate higher-clearance citizens on what can melt.

That is the origin behind the Molten Melted Labs & Drive-Thru in ECC Sector. Indigo and higher-clearance citizens would use the drive-thru to drop off a sample of anything. Then staff would use industrial-strength lasers to melt the sample, record the melting point and present both to the citizen (yes, this made sense to a Violet clearance leader, which is probably why he went from Chief Superintendent of IntSec in 17 sectors to Chief Inspector of ticketbots). The problem is how three such samples were accidentally turned into radioactive bombs that would create a nuclear explosion when hit, electrified or teased about their weight.

MATERIALS and METHODOLOGY

The Computer Ignition Facility used 192 lasers, each around 2.5 terawatts strong, in a giant circle around a sample levitating in magnetic confinement. When activated, it flash-boiled the outer layer of a sample so quickly that a pressure wave went inwards from all sides, compressing it so densely that it became an excellent fuel source for BrightHappyComplex-class nuclear reactors. Instead of mining for radioactive elements, this created them.

The Molten Melted Labs & Drive-Thru used the exact same setup to find the melting point of samples. Since the whole process takes around 0.75 nanoseconds, staff had to look up melting points in an old physics textbook and report that. This seemed pointless but considering how it mollified a citizen with enough authority to erase you from reality, the staff thought it a win.

INTENDED RESULTS

The goal of the labs was twofold: 1) Allow high-clearance citizens to test the melting point of any substance they have so nothing melts unexpectedly and 2) give Violet clearance citizens anything they wanted. This might not have led to saving all of Alpha Complex but it kept many Violet clearance citizens happy and that is basically the same thing.

ACTUAL RESULTS

As the R&D representatives in this team keep yelling, this project is technically not a failure. The 192 lasers did melt anything brought to the labs and the melting point was communicated through the drive-thru speakers. The sample was even returned through the drive-thru and only 12% of the staff were declared public enemies by Violet citizens and hunted down by Troubleshooters.

The problem (or more accurately problems, plural) was the samples being brought in. Used items normally found in Violet manors: Antique rugs, marble floor tiles, servants who forgot their place, that sort of thing. But three citizens – Shane-V-POC, Amanda-V-CAG and Mandy-V-ATA – brought in fissile materials. The laser compression almost caused these to enter nuclear fusion but since they did not explode like a nuclear warhead, they were sent through the drive-thru and back to the Violet citizens who took them home. In other words, three ambitious and powerful people had a radioactive nuke as a conversation piece.

Device: Power Services has named these Pre-Detonated Nuclear Whatsits (PDNW). They are the size and shape of a funball, weigh around 20kg and emit between 50–100 rads per hour. They are also unstable, so any powerful impact or energy discharge would create a 60-kiloton explosion. R&D likes to point out that this is less than half the yield of the Armed Forces' Herald of Death nuclear bomb, but those same R&D scientists would not be in the blast radius.

Response: Power Services detected the radiation spikes in ECC Sector and sent a Troubleshooter team to investigate (smartly leaving their personnel out of range). After some investigations, the team tracked down the Violet citizens in question and managed to retrieve all three PDNWs without too many clone replacements. Power Services safely disposed of them to avoid an accidental nuclear apocalypse. Or they are keeping them in a freezer. Either way, it is their problem now.

INDIVIDUALS OF NOTE

SHANE-V-POC

/// SKILLS

INTIMIDATE:	+4
BUREAUCRACY:	+3
CHARM:	-4

/// HEALTH BOXES

SHANE-V-POC ⬤⬤⬤⬤⬤⬤

/// NOTES

Some Violet citizens are delusional, paranoid master manipulators. Shane-V is also arrogant.

CARRYBOT DZ-R 4200 GTE
(AKA 'DOZER')

/// SKILLS

OPERATE:	+2
SCIENCE:	+5
CHARM:	-5

/// HEALTH BOXES

CARRYBOT DZ-R 4200 GTE ◯ ◯ ◯ ◯

/// NOTES

Dozer has three lead-lined internal storage containers for the rods. But the radiation is so strong, Dozer keeps losing its memory, including the memory of storing the rods inside it.

LOCATIONS OF NOTE
Drive-Thru, Molten Melted Labs

Almost all lower-clearance citizens travel through transbots, autohacks, their own two feet or the two feet of someone they can blackmail. That is why drive-thrus are so rare; only citizens of Green clearance or higher tend to have their own autocars. Citizens would drive up to a microphone, demand service from the losers working there and drop the sample they want melted into a one metre wide pneumatic tube. It is delivered straight to the labs, where it is immediately melted by the industrial lasers. Then staff read a textbook on melting points, guess what the sample is made from and sends what's left of the sample back along with a note stating the melting point. Sometimes, heavy samples get stuck and some lucky clone gets to climb inside and free it.

Special Actions

Violence + Athletics to avoid taking a Hurt from the giant pneumatic tube.
NODE +3 to convince staff to melt whatever you send through the tube,
including teammates.

EVIDENCE

> VIDEO SURVEILLANCE FOOTAGE, ECC SECTOR MOLTEN
> MELTED LABS DRIVE-THRU <A car with violet trim pulls into the
> drive-thru>
>
> **Shane-V-POC:** Hello? Service please! Or are you vat-headed
> yahoos sleeping on the job?
> **Lab Tech Keisha-Y:** Hello and welcome to Molten Melted Labs
> home of the melting any thing how can I help you?
> **Shane-V-POC:** Whatevs. Here, melt the crap out of this...
> whatever this stuff is.
> <The car's driver window opens. An arm extends to drop a rod
> made from plutonium-239 into the pneumatic tube.>
> **Lab Tech Keisha-Y:** Thank you one moment please... Citizen, do
> you mind pressing the Send button?
> **Shane-V-POC:** Boy, my ears must not work. Kinda sounded like you
> just gave me an order. Did I hear that right?
> <A door in the building opens. Out comes a Yellow-clearance lab
> tech who calmly walks up to the pneumatic tube and pressed the
> green Send button. Then she returns to the building.>
> **Lab Tech Keisha-Y:** Thank you, one moment please... This should
> only take about five minutes.
> **Shane-V-POC:** Weird. That's the same amount of time your
> execution would take.
> <Three minutes pass while the driver keeps honking the horn. The
> pneumatic tube shudders and the sample reappears looking
> more spherical.>
> **Lab Tech Keisha-Y:** Your melting point is 639.4 degrees. Now, we
> suggest you use lead-lined containers because this sample is highly...
> **Shane-V-POC:** Wait, that sounds a lot like another order. Are you
> really that over-medicated?
> **Lab Tech Keisha-Y:** ...My apologies, citizen. Have a great daycycle!

TROUBLESHOOTER ACTIVITY

Background: Here, the three Violet citizens already turned their samples into PDNWs and are at home deciding whether they go best on the mantelpiece or the 12-person dinner table. As they carried the samples home, radiation spikes were detected and Power Services alerted.

Act 1: Troubleshooters are briefed by Power Services personnel: Due to radiation spikes in ECC Sector, terrorists may be planting nuclear bombs in the area. Go to that sector, use the provided Geiger counters to locate the source of the spikes and safely disarm the devices. Since they do not know how to do that, each is given an instruction sheet. Because the instructions are Violet clearance, the entire sheet is blacked out. Once in ECC Sector, the counters direct the team to the Molten Melted Labs & Drive-Thru. Yellow clearance staff can be convinced (i.e. bribed) into revealing they gave three highly radioactive samples to the three Violet citizens.

Act 2: Either through personal initiative or Computer orders, the team must travel to each Violet citizen's manor and retrieve the samples without angering the citizens (stop laughing, it could happen). Shane-V-POC is not home so the team must convince his majordomo to permit them to leave with it. Amanda-V-CAG is home but having a lavish dinner party and assumes the Troubleshooters are the night's entertainment. Mandy-V-ATA is playing squash with her sample. Since the team has no special carrying cases, they must use their hands to carry the radioactive samples. Talk about hair loss, disorientation and nausea as their Moxie slowly bleeds away.

Act 3: Once the team has secured all three PDNWs, what do they do with them? Power Services gets upset if the team says there are no terrorist nukes, believing the team has turned traitor. Molten Melted Labs staff pretends the Troubleshooters do not exist. As for Friend Computer, it is surprisingly helpful at first, telling the team to bring all three PDNWs to the debriefing. Then Shane-V, pissed that someone swiped his conversation piece when he was not home, demands IntSec arrests the team for Grand Theft Art Thingie. Before the team gets arrested and then terminated or terminated and then arrested, a Power Services Nuclear Fuel Disposal Team arrives and offers to properly dispose of the PDNWs. Are these really experts or are they terrorists? That depends. Did the players bring enough snacks?

NUTRITIVE ANTI-MALWARE UPDATE 2.3M7

NO THANKS, I JUST DIDN'T EAT.

EXECUTIVE SUMMARY

Clones that do not eat have been a dream of resource officers and cafeteria janitors throughout Alpha Complex. The savings from such a development could be put toward any number of efficient and vital missions for Friend Computer and the happiness of every citizen. The R&D team in PCC Sector were the first ever to create such clones, with the uniquely ground-breaking Nutritive Anti-Malware Update 2.3 Mark 7 (NAMU 2.3m7). It overwrote perception and sensation codes in a citizen's iBall and Cerebral Coretech, transforming how they viewed food and sustenance.

The intent was not to create clones that did not eat but rather clones who viewed any technically edible foodstuff as delicious and desirable (yes, even Hearty-Hearty Brickloaf with Xtra Unidentified Crunchy Bits). NAMU 2.3m7 took it a step further and programmed every clone who received the update to lose the ability to recognise food.

MATERIALS and METHODOLOGY

The NAMU project has reported impressive results since its beginnings in the year 214. Although some created localised catastrophes, like NAMU1.1m2 and NAMU1.2m1, they have received average ratings of Excellent, Good Enough or Almost Harmless. NAMU2.2m3 received complex-wide accolades after 22.4% of test subjects experienced Cold Fun to be both cold and fun, a 129% improvement over previous tests.

Creating NAMU2.3m7 was a simple matter of copying and pasting code from NAMU2.2m3, NAMU 2.3m4 and the audio tracks from a recent Teela-O propaganda video, editing out the irrelevant operations and fine-tuning the rest. Upon completion, it was ready for launch using the standard upgrade, surveillance and memory capture package found in all Cerebral Coretech below Indigo clearance.

INTENDED RESULTS
Had it worked as designed, NAMU2.3m7 would have enabled Infrared and Red clearance clones to ingest sustenance from a wider spectrum of possible sources. For example, batches of discarded food from higher-clearance citizens (tested and confirmed to be more nutritive than the food served in Infrared cafeterias) could be delivered and picked over efficiently and with far less resource waste.

Further, it would allow Troubleshooters in the field, and any other citizens operating away from their cafeterias during mealtimes, to simply scan the area for items their bodies could conceivably break down into essential vitamins and minerals.

W A R N I N G

CITIZENS SHOULD NOT EAT THEIR REGULAR-SIZED FRIENDS. EATING FRIENDS IS TREASON, UNLESS YOU ARE EXPLICITLY ORDERED TO DO SO BY FRIEND COMPUTER, A HIGHER-CLEARANCE CITIZEN OR YOUR SUPERVISOR.

ACTUAL RESULTS
Had the R&D team checked with HPD&MC researchers on direct nervous system iBall/Coretech patching, they could have predicted that any alteration to what a clone considers delicious has unavoidable grave consequences. In this case, the patch did not just change the way recipients perceived food and identified sustenance. It made them forget about food as a concept, failing to perceive even delicious UV leftovers as something they could and should eat. They worked and lived without food until they dropped dead from malnutrition. As malnutrition is considered neglectful destruction of Computer property, those who starved were immediately arrested, tried and terminated.

To make matters worse, R&D communications tech 14th class Isiah-Y-PCC accidentally hit 'Reply All' rather than 'Reply' when sending Patch NAMU2.3m7 to initial test subjects. Instead of 144 Infrared clones receiving the update, it was sent to the entire Alpha Complex population. Only those in a dead zone, suffering from accidentally damaged iBalls or who had treasonously installed anti-updating software on their Cerebral Coretech were spared.

The problem was not immediately detected, as none of the impacted clones remembered the need for, or even the very concept, of food. They carried on with their daily lives, unaware that death was just a few weeks away. Many of those unaffected failed to notice at first, other than getting extra helpings of their favourite foods as supplies suddenly stopped running out. The first official mention of NAMU2.3m7's effects was in a pair of PLC reports one daycycle apart. The first bemoaned massive food wastage across all sectors, blaming the problem on poor sector management by people lower on the clearance ladder. The second took credit for a sudden reduction in food consumption throughout Alpha Complex thanks to people higher on the clearance ladder. Alert citizens in HPD&MC were able to piece the puzzle together in time to find a solution.

Device: Patch NAMU2.3m was written in the KOBOLD programming language and required 1.21 Gigaflops of available memory storage to install. Known firmware conflicts exist in 87.3% of iBall operating systems. Bots installed with Patch NAMU2.3m experienced visual hallucinations, condition errors and a softly undefined yearning. All known instances of the patch were ~~copied discreetly and saved in a file vault at PCC sector R&D headquarters~~ deleted at the end of the testing cycle.

Response: CPU improvised a temporary solution by installing a second patch over the top of NAMU2.3m7 that made recipients identify Hot Fun, Imitation Gagh Substitute and Bouncy Bubble Beverage Ultra as medications. Docbots then added recommended daycycle intake amounts of these 'meds' be added to their prescriptions. This was paired with the activation of several hundred Troubleshooters suffering from iBalls damaged in the line of duty, put to the task of force-feeding Infrared drones by the thousands. These two heroic measures kept enough clones sufficiently nourished until a team at HPD&MC uninstalled NAMU2.3m7 from the affected population. Only 45,312 citizens died of hunger, which is less than the infamous Arsenic Chewies incident (they were mostly Infrared anyway, so no paperwork was required).

ARCHIE-O-JRL

/// SKILLS

SCIENCE: +2

ENGINEER: +3

ALPHA COMPLEX: -2

/// HEALTH BOXES

ARCHIE-O-JRL ● ● ● ●

/// NOTES

This ranking officer of PCC Sector R&D has not eaten since the patch went live. He is ready to blame anyone nearby for his stomach pain and listlessness.

MILLIE-I-PCC

/// SKILLS

BLUFF: +4

BUREAUCRACY: +5

STEALTH: -3

/// HEALTH BOXES

MILLIE-I-PCC ● ● ● ● ● ●

/// NOTES

Millie-I is very excited about the resource savings represented by PCC sector no longer needing food. The extra XP Points in the budget will help her build a third submarine pen, this time in water.

LOCATIONS OF NOTE
The Dumpy Dump
Three days of continued food deliveries went out between NAMU2.3m7's advent and PLC's temporary cessation of deliveries. That food went entirely to rot (yes, even Hearty-Hearty Brickloaf with Xtra Unidentified Crunchy Bits) and was eventually carted off one scrubot load at a time to a disused warehouse in the lower levels of Sector HGL. The pile continues to rot even now in Year 214, its contents bubbling, outgassing and potentially alive (CPU did not agree with this possibility, but if we classify Infrareds as alive then a gigantic pile of rotting former food counts as well).

Special Actions
NODE +1 for Demolition rolls as it outgases various flammables and explosives on a regular basis.
NODE −1 for any social rolls since the pile of rotting food makes people want to flee, not listen.

//**/INTSEC SECURITY NOTE: There is not, never has been and never will be an entire sector in the Underplex populated entirely by clones fully loaded with the software, feeding directly off of their immediate environment. PCC Sector is not, never has been and never will be sending their toxic waste and depleted reactor fuel to that non-existent sector for fast, non-resource-intensive disposal. /**//

Recovery Node NAMU Alpha
Several hundred clones affected by NAMU2.3m7 were unable to uninstall the patch and now live in a sterile ward at the outskirts of PCC Sector. They are fed intravenously four times per daycycle and otherwise live fairly normal lives. The entire ward still receives normal food supply rations, which are kept in a larder for one day before being sold online.

Special Actions

NODE +1 for trading anything to receive food since the clones here do not value it.

NODE –3 for any conversation with the residents here since they are barely alive.

EVIDENCE

GROUP CHAT TRANSCRIPT

Millipede <Millie-I-PCC>: Yes! Guess what? Remember those R&D scientists I bought last year? They found a way to stop clones from needing food all the time! No bathroom breaks! No food costs! I gonna be rich!

OhNoNo <Lakshmi-I-PCD>: What's a food?

OhNoNo <Lakshmi-I-PCD>: And why does it cost XP Points?

FlunkieMonkey<Jen-I-RCF>: What she said.

WhatNameDoIUseHere <Carl-I-KID>: Food, huh? Never heard of it. Is it an old vehicle of some kind?

Millipede <Millie-I-PCC>: My mistake. I meant to type 'good'. They do not need good anymore. Mediocre will suffice for most issued goods. I'm going to save a fortune on requisitions.

TROUBLESHOOTER ACTIVITY

Background: The mission begins after the update's impact has just been discovered but before the 'medication' solution is implemented. While the update will go live throughout Alpha Complex, PCC Sector was the first. That is where the most starving, desperate and confused citizens can be found.

Act 1: In the mission briefing, the Troubleshooters are ordered to run a taste test in PCC Sector between Soylent Ruby, Soylent Crimson and battery acid. They are assigned three crates full of canned soylent of each flavour (yes, acid is a flavour now) and sent to PCC Sector's Buying Makes Me Happy Mall. Once there, every citizen refuses to taste anything, not even realising it is legally food. The Computer calls

with an important mission override: The team must find R&D Lab Team Punchbowl somewhere in PCC Sector, arrest them politely (they are all Yellow clearance) and force-feed them so they do not die of starvation before interrogation.

Act 2: Lab Team Punchbowl is still in its lab in a Yellow clearance R&D building. The team will need to get past security, search through the building (finding as many experimental devices as needed to create internecine warfare) and finally find the seven Yellow researchers. Once the surviving R&D team is fed (hopefully Soylent and not acid), IntSec finally arrives and takes them to nearby HAR Sector's Aggressive Interview Concourse.

Then Friend Computer has another lovely urgent override: Get the computer passwords of each researcher and upload the NAMU code to HPD&MC so they can reverse engineer a solution to mandatory starvation. Yes, the same scientists now in HAR Sector. The IntSec agents there will be absolutely pleased to see Troubleshooters. After getting the passwords, the team witnesses severe starvation in everywhere PCC Sector. That's when half the team gets the update and can no longer recognise food. When they reach the lab, they find security has been severely improved since a group of Red citizens recently got inside.

Act 3: Before the team can use the passwords, Protocol Officer Millie-I-PCC arrives looking happy. She noticed a sharp reduction in food costs since NAMU2.3m7 was released and has issued an order to keep it going indefinitely so she can pocket the savings. She immediately orders the team to leave. Once outside, Friend Computer will send the 2nd Non-Volunteer Assault Regiment to 'support' the Troubleshooters to get back in there, use the passwords and upload the data needed to save everyone. Too bad the Assault Regiment is armed with grenades, artillery and flameshooters. You know, the kind of stuff that could ruin a hard drive.

ORESCOPE (NOW IN SOUNDICOLOUR!)

WATCH YOUR STEP. NO, WATCH ALL OF THEM.

EXECUTIVE SUMMARY

Alpha Complex has been running low on available resources since Year 214 and current models predict shortages will appear for lower-clearance citizens as soon as ERROR_DATE_NEGATIVE. HPD&MC and PLC both approached R&D to develop a better system of spotting valuable ores such as copper, iron and fluoride. (PLC wanted more raw materials for their factories, while HPD&MC did not want to build another block of flats on top of a lead deposit for fear The Computer will have the building destroyed and then tell HPD&MC to build a swimming pool in the empty space.)

R&D soon began Project Visible Ore Not Visible (VONV) to create the Orescope. The typical ground-penetrating radar unit uses radio waves but this interfered with local bot communications. Therefore, 400 Infrareds were trained through educational shocks to scream loudly on command. The sonar waves they created revealed valuable ore deposits. An unscheduled earthquake proved that Orescope exacerbated pre-existing conditions in fault lines. Thankfully, the only people terminated were wanted terrorists.

MATERIALS and METHODOLOGY

Originally, the R&D team responsible for Project VONV had only requested the following: a large funnel, four rolls of duct tape, a 3D spectrum analyser, a top-of-the-line media player, a very big speaker and rights to use the song 'Drop It Like It's Hot (Enough To Cause 2nd-Degree Burns)'. The plan was to tape the funnel to the speaker, balance the small end on some exposed rock and play the song. Then they would measure the echoes and use that to render a 3D model of whatever is trapped inside the rock.

Experiments #001 through #006 proved to be failures, so the team did some research and discovered ground-penetrating radar uses radio waves, not sound. Then they created K-SLAB, a radio station beaming its signal (and Top 40 Loyal Hits) down into the stony ground. Days later, they realised nothing was catching the echoes when no one called during the Get The Lead Out programme on Thursday's morning zoo show Morning Glory with Chipper-Y and Very Stupid Traitor.

By now, the expected budget overruns were getting big enough to notice, so project manager Theresa-G-CAS opted for a new strategy. Borrowing 400 Infrared citizens from a nearby Rest 'n' Work Harder Mandatory Efficiency Improvement Break Room, Theresa-G had all 400 scream in unison at a local slab of rock. That did nothing, so they added a 120,000-watt amplifier typically used in Acoustic Negative Reinforcement Therapy. This time, they remembered to include equipment to project the results on a vidscreen in full colour.

INTENDED RESULTS

At the successful conclusion of this project, R&D would have created a device that directed energy waves into the rock surrounding Alpha Complex and read the resulting echoes to identify valuable ore deposits, aquifers and treasure chests. This would have increased available metals and minerals by an average of 230%, helping usher in a new era of bountiful plenty for Alpha Complex and removing at least 12 different triggers for treasonously hoarding resources. Now armed with ample supplies, Armed Forces, Internal Security and even Troubleshooters could take the fight to the terrorists and defeat them through sheer attrition. The Orescope would have saved all of Alpha Complex from the terrorist menace once and for all, thanks entirely to R&D.

ACTUAL RESULTS

When all 400 Infrareds were shown a Teela-O video where she seductively removes a floppy hat, the resulting sound wave post-amplification measured above 335 decibels. R&D was not ready to capture such loud data and everyone in the team was deafened while three died due to brain haemorrhages. (Infrareds were also harmed in the making of this project but who cares about that?)

Once the team accounted for such volume, they captured the data and identified new sources of skarn and nickel for PLC to mine. However, the massive sound waves created an acoustic fluidisation within three unidentified fault lines. The subsequent earthquakes swallowed PRL Sector entirely at a loss of 32,855 citizens, 542 citizens that actually matter and, worst of all, several paintings created by High Programmer Bruce-U-NMN considered extremely valuable by people who like their limbs still attached.

That would have been bad enough but R&D forgot to give the Infrared citizens their daily meds. As the Focusol, Thymoblandin and assorted hormone suppressants faded, the crowd grew rowdy (among other growths). Their complaining and grunting triggered more earthquakes and threatened to destroy all of Alpha Complex.

Device: The Orescope uses sonar to identify materials buried deep within rock. The main device is roughly the size of a scrubot and has two large cables: One to connect to a funnel-like sound collector the size of a confession booth and another room-sized funnel. The user causes a loud sound to go into the collector, which is then amplified up to 340 decibels (heads literally explode around 240 dB, so be careful). A nearby monitor displays the results in colourful 3D renderings called 'Soundicolour'.

Response: A Troubleshooter team was dispatched to investigate. It discovered that all 33,397 residents of PRL Sector were terrorists plotting against The Computer. R&D somehow knew this and created the experiment to help dispatch all those traitors. Yet the Orescope continued to send massive sound waves into the ground, creating more earthquakes and collateral damage. Eventually, IntSec arrived with enough firepower to destroy all traitors and the 400 screaming Infrareds. The Orescope was mothballed until earthquakes become fashionable.

INDIVIDUAL OF NOTE

THERESA-G-CAS

/// SKILLS

SCIENCE:	+5
PROGRAM:	+3
CHARM:	-4

/// HEALTH BOXES

THERESA-G-CAS ● ● ●

/// NOTES

Really good working with science, really bad working with humans. After using the Orescope, she has trouble hearing. Yes, that will be the Troubleshooter's fault.

LOCATION OF NOTE

The PRL Sector Chasm

This is a giant, deep chasm opened up by the Orescope's earthquake. PRL Sector was above it; now it lies in ruins at the bottom. Rebar, sparking wires, collapsed walls and dead citizens are abundant down there but that is a good 150 metres down. A few survivors could still be trying to eke out an existence there, free from The Computer and silly things like working plumbing or tarts without so much as a rat in them.

Special Actions

NODE +1 for climbing into the chasm since the walls are full of cracks and ledges.

NODE −1 for climbing back up because heading down caused the cracks and ledges to weaken.

All of PRL Sector (at least what's left of it) is a dead zone.

EVIDENCE

INTSEC NON-AGGRESSIVE QUESTIONING TRANSCRIPT

Theresa-G: What's important here is how the Orescope discovered several rich ore deposits beneath PRL Sector.

IntSec Agent: You mean atop and even inside PRL Sector now.

Theresa-G: Yes, so it's even easier to mine! I found it and made it easy to reach. Ta da!

IntSec Agent: What about the 30,000-plus dead citizens?

Theresa-G: What about them?

IntSec Agent: Some were above your clearance.

Theresa-G: Didn't you read the Troubleshooters' report? All those citizens were traitors in cahoots with each other. I have the XP Point receipts proving the Troubleshooters reported that.

IntSec Agent: Oh, right. Hey, what is a 'cahoot' anyway?

Theresa-G: No clue but those PRL Sector traitors had cahoots up to their eyeballs!

IntSec Agent: But somehow, your 400 Infrared volunteers survived.

Theresa-G: Yeah, about that...

TROUBLESHOOTER ACTIVITY

Background: This mission starts soon after the Orescope caused an earthquake but before it was dismantled. PRL Sector lies in ruins at the bottom of the chasm.

Act 1: PRL Sector stopped communicating entirely at 14:50:12 yesterdaycycle. The mission is to find it and bring it back online for normal communications. Each Troubleshooter is outfitted with standard rock climbing gear and noise-cancelling headphones for some reason. There aren't enough for all Troubleshooters, so one will go without gear or headphones. Let the players argue that one out.

Act 2: Once they arrive, they see PRL Sector was swallowed by an earthquake and rests roughly 150 metres down a large chasm. A now-mostly-deaf Theresa-G-CAS is waiting for them by the Orescope and 400 grumbling Infrareds. She offers a deal: If the team reports that the entire sector was overrun by traitors and helps her create fake evidence of that, each Troubleshooter will be promoted to Orange clearance – except one chosen by the team, who becomes Infrared and a scapegoat. Once reported back, The Computer fully believes the team who must now terminate 33,397 traitors with Coretech video evidence. There are also several large ore deposits, one made from nickel and the other from skarn, which can earn the team 500 XP Points if reported (and angering Theresa-G who wants the credit).

Act 3: The Troubleshooters will have to climb down into PRL Sector's ruins to get evidence they were even there, then deal with 11 survivors who are 1) Orange clearance and 2) very cross right now, thank you. Once there, the Infrareds start complaining about local funball teams and mini-earthquakes keep recurring. Finally back to the surface, the Troubleshooters receive demands from the Infrareds for funball swag or they will scream again. If the Troubleshooters do not deal with this, an army of IntSec agents arrives to terminate everyone there. Yes, everyone.

Note: If the Disaster Deck is available, take out the Earthquake card and give it to the Troubleshooter most likely to use it. Once used, take it back. Then discreetly hand it to whichever player got hurt the most by the first earthquake.

PCPUFIX

THIS IS FINE. EXCEPT MY FORMS ARE ON FIRE

EXECUTIVE SUMMARY

Paper forms are classified as a strategic resource for Alpha Complex. Without them, the system would grind to a halt. A single sector will go through a tonne or more of paper per day. While digital forms exist and see wide use, they are vulnerable to power outages, packet loss, hackers and bit rot (plus, only Ultraviolet clearance citizens can view the source code and no one is brave enough to ask for their coding help). Paper hard copies, while not invulnerable, are simply more reliable. The difficulty is that the materials to make new paper are increasingly scarce and recycling used forms is yielding diminishing returns as recyclable material is lost to fire, theft, decomposition and wastebasket funball tournaments.

CPU managed to find the one R&D scientist in all of Alpha Complex who is obsessively interested in the subject of paperwork optimisation. Peggy-Y-HES designed the Paper CPU Form Indexing eXpediter

(PCPUFIX), a hanger-sized, fully automated form processing system that could be installed in a CPU Form Processing & Handwriting Mockery Centre in WEH Sector. The design was sound on paper (ahem) but kept changing as construction on the prototype progressed to keep up with new CPU directives and stakeholder demands. When activated, faults in the system created a backup of paper forms that grew to mountainous size, burst its containment and threatened to bury the whole sector with no signs of stopping.

MATERIALS AND METHODOLOGY

Start with a flow chart illustrating the requirements, checks and processes of each form in a system. Then build a version of it in metal using conveyor belts and optical scanners. Automate everything using customised bots that run on rails throughout the system. The result is immensely complex and immensely expensive but workable. A proof of concept version was successfully demonstrated on Form HPDMC-2758-EZ (Survey of Citizen Attitudes About Forms). The trial was then scaled up. Due to the frequent changes in directives, conveyor belts were made to be reconfigurable on the fly, able to move, expand and contract into new positions.

INTENDED RESULTS

For years, the bulk of CPU operations have been done by clones sitting at desks checking stacks of forms. For something so vital to Alpha Complex, we can do so much better. Combined with reforms to CPU procedures to eliminate redundancies from the system, thousands of clones can be freed from desk work, forms can be processed more quickly, errors and treasons can be found more quickly and overall treason will even go down! Such a system would also allow less waste and lost forms, reduce the need for keeping vast form inventories and saving large quantities of paper (real, recycled, double recycled and two-ply).

ACTUAL RESULTS

3,982 tonnes of paper were lost in the breach of the PCPUFIX facility, including some to fire. Business in WEH Sector collapsed and slowed in three nearby sectors as rooms, hallways and citizen's lungs filled with fresh paper forms. Although the device would have run out of paper before filling all of Alpha Complex, the loss of forms and work would ripple through the complex, leading to unacceptable and dangerous levels of higher-clearance citizen annoyance.

Device: PCPUFIX is a warehouse-sized labyrinthine mess of conveyor belts, custom bots on rails, optical scanners and, for some reason, tubas that only its creator understands (and that much is questionable). Then there are the Stacks, the storage for clean paper forms and their backups, where bots take and place paper so quickly that some forms smoulder.

Response: In response to some early problems in the system, a Troubleshooter team was employed as problem-solving muscle to assist Peggy-Y in tuning the system. During that mission, PCPUFIX had its critical malfunction. Investigations are ongoing as to whom can be blamed for it but blaming Troubleshooters has 1:1.5 odds. Peggy-Y (with some backing from R&D higher-ups) and Jayden-G-SKD (the CPU coordinator for the project) are each accusing each other of sabotage. Neither has suggested blaming the Troubleshooter team yet but that has 1:1 odds.

INDIVIDUALS OF NOTE

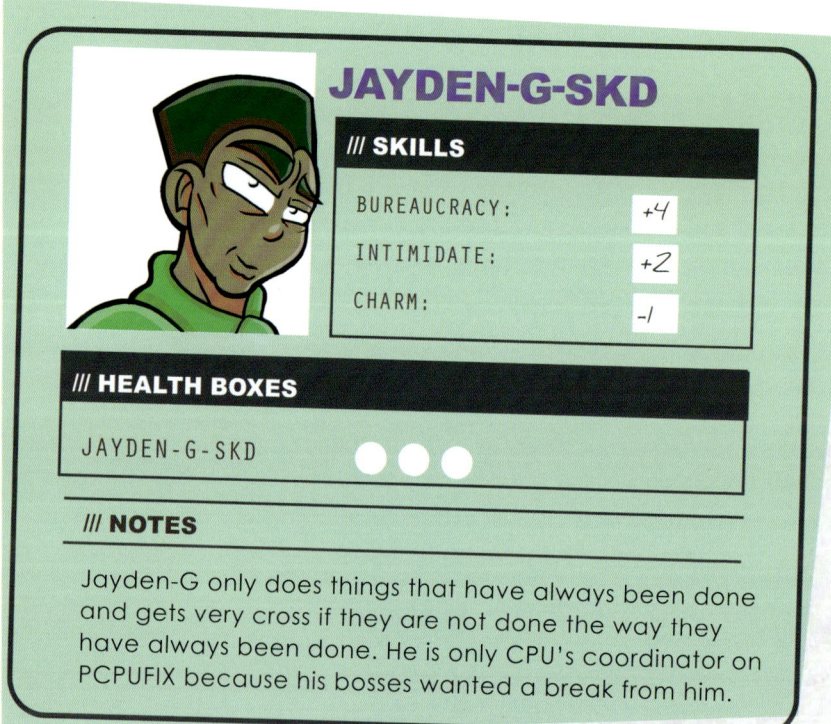

JAYDEN-G-SKD

/// SKILLS

BUREAUCRACY:	+4
INTIMIDATE:	+2
CHARM:	-1

/// HEALTH BOXES

JAYDEN-G-SKD ● ● ●

/// NOTES

Jayden-G only does things that have always been done and gets very cross if they are not done the way they have always been done. He is only CPU's coordinator on PCPUFIX because his bosses wanted a break from him.

PEGGY-Y-HES

/// SKILLS

BUREAUCRACY: +4

PROGRAM: +2

ATHLETICS: -2

/// HEALTH BOXES

PEGGY-Y-HES ⚪ ⚪

/// NOTES

An idea person with a simmering resentment of Jayden-G. Has not been thrown under the transbot yet because no one else can do what she does and she knows how to store blackmail material on co-workers.

LOCATION OF NOTE
PCPUFIX Warehouse
This project takes up a large warehouse within CPU's Central Form Processing & Handwriting Mockery Centre. Completed forms ride around on conveyor belts that use strong suction to hold the papers in place (a clone walking along them will need to make some rolls to avoid getting stuck). The conveyor belts sometimes move between different endpoints. Bots with long but delicate arms move forms around the various stations including scanning, printing and 'Need A Good Laugh' bins. Rejected forms are sent to a huge mechanical shredder with great gnashing teeth. There are a few offices adjacent and a large paper storage area.

Special Actions
NODE +1 to requisition extra equipment, since all the forms are right here.
NODE –1 to avoid setting paper on fire.

EVIDENCE

TROUBLESHOOTER ACTIVITY

Background: The mission starts before PCPUFIX has started but not reached its catastrophic malfunction. Higher-ups in CPU are fed up with Peggy-Y and are looking for dirt on her; other than casual connections with ACLHG, Peggy-Y is squeaky clean. (Better put, Peggy-Y is very good at hiding her crimes.)

Act 1: The Troubleshooters are briefed by Jayden-G-SKD, a Green clearance bureaucrat from CPU. Peggy-Y-HES, the designer of PCPUFIX, is suspected of treason but The Computer prefers to see actual evidence against a Yellow clearance citizen. As cover, the Troubleshooters are to assist Peggy-Y in improving the efficiency of PCPUFIX. They are given a digital access key to her makeshift office in the warehouse; they can use it without getting in trouble with The Computer but are warned they will not be protected if they are caught by anyone else because that would ruin their undercover operation.

Act 2: On arriving at the PCPUFIX Warehouse, Peggy-Y insists on confiscating the Troubleshooter's laser pistols, citing fire risk (same goes for any other fire risks she catches them with). They are stored in a locker in her temporary office inside a broom closet. The task she sets them on involves clearing the small mountain of backed-up paper in one section of the device and tracking down the source of the problem that created it. Attempts to service the machine without proper forms (which Peggy-Y can issue) will be stopped by the bots running on rails around and through the machine. Any damage to the machine will cause another paper backup. Inevitably, the Troubleshooters will do something to anger Peggy-Y, at which point she stops cooperating with them until they are sufficiently contrite.

Inside her office is a non-networked desktop system that holds blackmail on Jayden-G working with Communists – and video of each Troubleshooter working with their own Secret Societies. Copies can be made but since it is not networked, the evidence cannot be uploaded to Friend Computer just yet (if the Troubleshooters never get inside the office, Peggy-Y will be called away to have more arguments with CPU about the PCPUFIX plans.) Just after someone finds her blackmail files, Jayden-G will contact the Troubleshooters for a progress report. Without saying anything explicitly incriminating, he hints at a big promotion if they 'produce' evidence against Peggy-Y one way or another.

Act 3: By now, literal mountains of paperwork are spilling out of the warehouse and burying the entire centre. Then paper landslides start to fill up everywhere in WEH Sector and elsewhere. Peggy-G panics, loudly denounces the team for whatever they did to create this mess and demands they fix it before she needs to execute the team for treason. Doing so is a dance of swinging conveyor belts into new positions, dodging grumpy bots and possible death by a landslide of paper cuts. Eventually this cuts the power and the system's bots start carrying lit candles to see in the darkness. Yes, open flames near a paper tsunami. If the team does not solve this, The Computer will send in a fleet of recyclebots: Zamboni-sized threshers pulping paper and anything that gets in their way.

PROJECT AMPLE

ARE YOU USING THESE? BECAUSE NOW I AM.

EXECUTIVE SUMMARY

Despite optimistic projections by PLC for the 12-year period between Year 214 and Year 214, available resources for continued operations in Alpha Complex have become increasingly strained. Fortunately, alert historians working for the R&D Old Stuff We Do Not Understand Anymore Division encountered an ancient practice called Reduce-Recycle-Regatta (experts suggest the last term means 'take things apart and use those parts to build other stuff'). This concept calls for production using materials already used (instead of finding new sources of materials) and is totally different than the previous 113 recycling mandates.

R&D created the Project AMPLE ('Another Method of Production Leveraging something that starts with E'), in which they programmed a handful of jackobots to scavenge resources from nearby scrap piles and turn what ordinary citizens consider garbage into serviceable equipment, weaponry, bots and possibly safe foodstuffs. The jackobots worked with extraordinary efficiency, completely beating even the most optimistic projections for how much material they would regatta into various complete and sellable goods.

This had the added benefit of identifying citizens suffering from insufficient awareness, slow crisis-management skills or a treasonous inability to flee quickly. Some 42,441 clones were regatted during

AMPLE's inaugural and only run. Near the end of the experiment, the jackobots began building an enormous robot from everything they could get their oily gripper claws on to create AMPLEBot Prime. (R&D scientists have yet to identify the programming that initiated this event but plan on blaming Red clearance employees as soon as some start complaining of working conditions.)

MATERIALS and METHODOLOGY

Older model jackobots were chosen for Project AMPLE for two reasons. First, they were significantly easier to come by than the newer, more powerful models. Second, their internal hard drives are ~~easier to hack~~ more suitable for R&D exploitation. The team used jackobots because they represented the best balance of useful tools and flexible task direction needed for a Reduce-Recycle-Regatta operation.

Despite the more accessible hard drives, the trickiest part of executing the project was overcoming the original protocol programming. It was more difficult than anticipated to get a jackobot to view a ruined laser pistol as anything other than a ruined laser pistol or an Infrared drone as anything other than a pitiful, cheap-to-replace sack of meat and red juice. The problem stumped the team for several daycycles until they came up with an ingenious solution.

Piggybacking on a software virus known to affect older jackobot models, R&D tacked the AMPLE protocols in place of the malicious code and set it to work inside 233 jackobots and watch what happened from a secure bunker. With AMPLE directives now driving the bots' decision-making protocols, they quickly set to work making useful objects out of sector refuse.

INTENDED RESULTS

The project sought to provide five key benefits as compared to the traditional Alpha Complex modes of equipment production:

- **Alertness** for opportunities to disassemble broken or used items.
- **Maximized** utility for every molecule of Computer property (i.e. everything).
- **Perfecting** the perfect utopia that is life in Alpha Complex by ending supply shortages forever.
- **Learning** to Reduce-Recycle-Regatta as part of everydaycycle life.
- **Explaining** what regatta means.

(R&D has been fined for violating mandate CP4401/b and assigning two definitions to the AMPLE acronym.)

Combining these five key elements was to start with jackobots but once proof of concept succeeded, it would expand programming for other bots and individual training from Infrared clearance on upward to Red clearance. The entirety of Alpha Complex could maximise its resource efficiency with one brilliant program!

ACTUAL RESULTS

Any competent bot mechanic from Technical Services would have spotted the hole in this plan immediately. Jackobots are built to be adaptable and resourceful. Within seconds of beginning their assignment, several of the test bots concluded they could complete their tasks far more quickly with the help of additional bots. They transmitted their virus to all other jackobots in XCL Sector. It soon spread to all bots of every kind in the area, then into those in adjacent sectors. As the code degraded from random upload errors, the bots began to Reduce-Recycle-Regatta not just trash but unattended equipment, sector furniture, walls, ductwork and slow-to-move citizens (yes, clone body parts were taken). External communication for XCL Sector was compromised almost immediately as the jackobots regatted the components for their new leader, AMPLEbot Prime.

Sector security could not call for help because the data lines were missing. Most citizens died in noble service to The Computer, either through fighting the compromised bot threat or through involuntarily sacrificing their bodies to a project (i.e. they did not run fast enough) and their parts added to AMPLEbot Prime. Only Kevin-R-XCL managed to escape by disguising himself as a jackobot (made from cardboard and aluminium foil). A team of Troubleshooters found him before the jackobots could reduce the team into bloody spare parts but because they still had working Coretechs, the jackobots piggybacked on their signals saying only, 'Send more Troubleshooters'.

More Troubleshooter teams arrived in XCL Sector, only to be regatted by AMPLEbot Prime's jackobots. 17 teams were massacred (as was the Armed Forces 55th Jackobot Cavalry Battalion, which in hindsight should not have been sent in). Eventually, Troubleshooters detonated an EMP bomb and saved Alpha Complex.

Device: Had AMPLEBot Prime's construction not been stopped, it would have been the largest engine of destruction ever unleashed on the happy citizens of Alpha Complex. Over 200 metres wide and made from bits of machinery, circuit boards and unwary citizens of XCL Sector, it had the appearance of a gigantic, sprawling jackobot. Nobody knows what damage it would have inflicted if left to grow.

Response: It took an embarrassing, not to say treasonous, number of missions before leadership in Tech Services and R&D realised the calls for help were traps laid by the virus. After this, a multilateral commission of Crisis Command Clone Professionals from PLC, HPD&MC and IntSec convened to devise a three-pronged approach to containing the catastrophe. IntSec responded by the minimal force necessary (currently labelled as 'pitiless'). PLC sent in a wave of hardened farradaybots to jam signals and slow the virus's spread. HPD&MC commissioned several Troubleshooter teams to infiltrate XCL Sector in hopes they would at least blow the whole thing up.

INDIVIDUAL OF NOTE

KEVIN-R-XCL

/// SKILLS

ATHLETICS:	+2
PSYCHOLOGY:	-3
STEALTH:	+5

/// HEALTH BOXES

KEVIN-R-XCL   ● ● ●

/// NOTES

Kevin escaped his sector and brought initial word of the catastrophe to security forces in neighbouring RXT Sector. He has gone quite mad and has developed severe anxiety over trash bins.

LOCATION OF NOTE
The Big Empty
By the time the virus was contained and all infected bots repurposed, memory wiped and buried in signal-resistant containers at the bottom of the MTN Sector salt mines, they had collected all matter in a half kilometre sphere surrounding what was originally XCL Sector headquarters. This region, now the largest dead zone in Alpha Complex, was never repaired or restocked. It echoes, vast and dark and empty, as a warning to loyal citizens. Also, it would have cost a lot of XP Points.

Special Actions
NODE −2 for any attempt to find supplies or find a citizen. The place is empty and hollow.

NODE +2 for hiding and subterfuge. It's a dark, creepy, abandoned dead zone.

EVIDENCE

COMMAND LOG PLURAL C ALPHA//R&D CONFESSIONS SPECIALIST PETE-I-GOL RE: AMPLE TEAM LEAD KIM-B-TTU
It must be noted that at no time did R&D's Kim-R-TTU (previously Kim-B-TTU) or his subordinates actively believe their efforts would cause the wasteful deaths of several tens of thousands of Infrared clones and thus they should be forgiven most of the shame, ignominy and summary punishment so many citizens wish to heap upon them. However, it must also be noted that Kim-R's decisions also caused the unscheduled termination of many dozens of high-clearance officials. This cannot be forgiven. It is my recommendation he be admitted to the Dr. Docbot Home for Wayward Traitors where he will be lovingly rehabilitated until dead.

TROUBLESHOOTER ACTIVITY
Background: This mission starts when the AMPLE virus spreads throughout XCL Sector but before it reaches much farther. Almost all citizens in the sector are... uh, disassembled and while the infrastructure is still there, most objects have become part of AMPLEbot Prime. The Computer does not yet know what is happening but it has received innocent calls from several jackobots reporting a dangerous shortage of everything.

Act 1: In the briefing, the Troubleshooters are told that XCL Sector is running low on several key resources, so the team will escort a truckbot full of supplies (most of the truckbot is full of metal and electronic parts but there is also a small fission reactor complete with half a plutonium rod). They have to get at least an Orange clearance citizen to sign receipts for all of the supplies. As the enter the sector, the team cannot find anyone. One jackobot per Troubleshooter comes over and offers to take the supplies off their hands. Then they try to disassemble the Troubleshooters. (Hey, parts is parts.)

Act 2: The Computer orders the team to find Kevin-R-XCL, who is the only resident left alive in the sector, and interrogate him to discover what is really going on. Kevin-R has lost it permanently and bounces between fleeing in fear and grabbing Troubleshooters by the shirt to tell them about the 'Big Bot Conspiracy'. Then the players see another Troubleshooter team just before they are literally torn apart by Frankensteining jackobots. Fleeing the bloodthirsty jackobots (or their clone replacements finally getting smart and running), they encounter the massive AMPLEbot Prime and either listen to its villain monologue about its plans or they run away again. By now, even the walls are being torn down, collapsing the floors above and providing more parts to collect. The Computer orders the team to retreat to neighbouring ROR Sector and team up with an Armed Forces battalion and lead them into battle. Turns out this force rides on jackobots like cavalry and no one will listen to the Troubleshooters about the virus. Oh dear.

Act 3: Once the soldier's mounts tear their humans apart, a few surviving solders escape with an EMP bomb. They plan on taking it to AMPLEbot Prime and detonating it. The team must escort them through a rapidly destabilising sector. Along the way, the soldiers all die, leaving the Troubleshooters to detonate the bomb. Too bad they do not have the detonation code ('w00t').

PROZAK WORKPLACE SOUNDTRACK

NO. TIME. FOR. WORK. MUST. LISTEN.

PROZAK WORKPLACE SOUNDTRACKEXECUTIVE SUMMARY

Observations indicate that the ambient environment can affect productivity, positively or negatively, by almost 150%. R&D researchers were thus tasked with creating the perfect soundtrack codenamed 'Prozak' to promote a state of joyous loyalty and fevered focus in low-clearance assembly line workers.

Implementation on volunteers from OEI Sector's Technical Services Battery Taste Test Centre at first indicated positive results, with an indication of strong stimulation to areas of subjects' brains. Following a general release, evidence showed terrorist sabotage had resulted in lowering productivity to effectively zero. Those responsible were swiftly terminated and the music was most likely deleted. Meh, let's say it was deleted for sure and head home early.

MATERIALS and METHODOLOGY

The objective assigned to the research team was to create an ambient soundtrack, which would best produce a positive and productivity-boosting response. This is based on the Uroboros Effect: Happy citizens work hard; hard working citizens become loyal; and loyal citizens become happy. Data modelling was used to ascertain effects that would stimulate the correct regions of the lower-clearance brain while avoiding the really stupid regions.

Workgroups of Infrared and Red citizens volunteered by their supervisors were placed in soundproofed rooms and scanned with brainwave monitors as Prozak test tracks were played. Additionally, the groups were asked to perform various tasks based on standard workline procedures identified as poor motivation-inducers, such as tweezer-assisted relocation of iron filings, counting pills in bottles without opening them and polishing fruit to be served at high-clearance banquets until they could see their faces in it (and without juicing).

Tests were performed using four potential Prozak workplace soundtracks dubbed Alpha, Beta, Theta and Rupert, with each tested on a different randomly-selected group. For the sake of control, a fifth group was exposed to an ambience mixing the four samples whilst a sixth was tasked to work with only the usual factory noises (HVAC, dropped metal, distance screams that suddenly cut off, etc.).

INTENDED RESULTS
A successfully developed optimal soundtrack would have resulted in a notable increase in productivity among workers. Consequent to this, the efficiency of projects taking place in pilot sectors would be boosted to the highest possible level, with gradual rollout throughout Alpha Complex leading to a golden age of both research and production, all thanks to the underpaid and underpromoted R&D staff. This would inevitably lead to the eradication of inefficiency and treason, the quashing of the last remaining vestiges of terrorist groups and R&D staff getting more XP Points.

ACTUAL RESULTS
Groups Alpha, Beta and Rupert each saw marginal if anecdotal effects on productivity, as well as marginal if anecdotal side-effects such as migraines, vomiting, hysteria, cranial haemorrhaging and believing they were someone called Ethel Merman. Effects on group Theta exceeded expectations, resulting in what might best be described as a state of 'drugged-out bliss without the drugs'. Unfortunately, the happiness level were so high that productivity was reduced to zero, with test subjects showing no interest in activities other than continued listening, even after the cessation of playback.

Making matters worse, certain test subjects displayed a strong, almost zealous, desire to let others hear the soundtrack. After test group Theta convinced a lab technician to listen to a sample, a chain reaction was set in place. Within a short time the entire research group had been exposed, followed swiftly by the entire lab. From there, the entire populace of the subsector was gradually exposed, with commandeered bots and media sources used to spread the Prozak to the wider sector.

Left unchecked, the results would have been a catastrophic total efficiency loss, resulting in everyone slowly dying of dehydration or starvation and the collapse of all systems including life support and CompNodes due to a total lack of maintenance.

Device: The Prozak workplace soundtrack is a carefully curated and created list of digital songs but without lyrics, proper instruments or sense of musical ability. Sample songs include the classic hit 'You're The Reason Why The Computer Cries', modern tunes such as 'Take Your Damn Pills Already (Reprise)' and the immortal 'Shoop Diddy Wop Ekke Ekke Ptang Zoo Boing'. Although popular, each was run through an audio-cranial code called the Algor-Rhythm to adjust the resulting sound waves to stimulate parts of the brain that need stimulating to allow management to increase production quotas for the 12th time this monthcycle.

Response: Troubleshooters were dispatched to ascertain the reason for a reduction of activity, swiftly identifying Prozak as the cause (so swiftly, we recommend aggressive questioning). Vulture Squadron was dispatched to neutralise and destroy all vectors of transmission, equipped with the most powerful noise-cancelling technology Armed Forces can supply and Algor-Rhythm source code transported to a secure isolated vault until such time as they might be weaponised against the enemies of Alpha Complex. Saboteurs in the R&D project team were identified, transferred to Power Services and promptly terminated.

LOCATION OF NOTE
Technical Services Battery Taste Test Centre
This is where TechServ personnel lick old batteries to see how much power is still in them. There is a soundproof room (leaking batteries still need to be licked) containing various workstations and a decent sound system because sometimes management uses this room for... fact-finding committee meetings that certainly do not involve experimental drugs or gambling. That might be why R&D got Tech Services to offer this centre for free.

INDIVIDUALS OF NOTE

MAJOR EDGAR-B-TVG

/// SKILLS

SCIENCE:	-+3
INTIMIDATE:	+4
DEMOLITIONS:	-2

/// HEALTH BOXES

MAJOR EDGAR-B-TVG ● ● ● ● ●

/// NOTES

Armed Forces leader responsible for new weapon development and testing. When he heard about what is going on in OEJ Sector, he literally ran here to get Prozak as 'his' latest invention.

SMAK TEAM MEMBERS

/// SKILLS

STEALTH:	+5
DEMOLITIONS:	+4
SCIENCE:	-5

/// HEALTH BOXES

SMAK TEAM MEMBERS ● ● ● ● ●

/// NOTES

SMAK team members are well trained in combat, demolitions, stealth and not caring about innocent bystanders.

Special Actions

+2 NODE to jury-rigging technical solutions using equipment in the workstation.

EVIDENCE

Kyle-Y: Group Theta test subject interview number one. Present are the unnamed test subject, project supervisor Kyle-Y-RCD and technician team lead Gary-O-RZQ, formally Gary-Y before I reported his complaints about our supervisor to our supervisor. Gary-O is now glaring at me.

Test Subject: Hey friend, I have a name. It's Barry-R. Good to meet you!

Kyle-Y: Don't care. Our reports show that you just sat around doing nothing instead of your assigned task to break down surplus graphite rods. Care to explain?

Test Subject: Who needs work, friend? We've got better things to do, you know?

Kyle-Y: No, no I don't know. Why don't you explain exactly what your group found that was so much better than work?

Gary-O: Hold on, I'll get the door.

Kyle-Y: Let it be noted for the recording that Gary-O has answered the door to a knocking technician Nicky-R who also used to be Yellow clearance before he complained about two supervisors.

Nicky-R: Guys, you gotta listen to this scrubot!

Gary-O: Can it wait until we finish this debriefing or do you want to be Infrared clearance?

Nicky-R: It's all good, friend! But you HAVE to hear this. Right now!

Gary-O: Is that a speaker array? What's going [PROZAK INTENSIFIES] ohhhhhh.

Kyle-Y: Ohhhhhh.

Test Subject: Oh? Sorry, I meant ohhhhh.

TROUBLESHOOTER ACTIVITY

Background: The mission starts shortly after an initial Troubleshooter team was sent to investigate and promptly fell victim to the Prozak.

Act 1: A Troubleshooter team sent to OEI Sector has failed to report back and is suspected of turning terrorist. The Troubleshooters are to ascertain their fate and complete their mission to investigate loss of efficiency across the sector. They are assigned a set of earplugs each, which allow communication between team members thanks to an iBall link but will

block out all other outside noise entirely – if they want to communicate with anybody not on their team, they will need to remove them or find a method of nonverbal communication. On arrival at the sector, the Troubleshooters run into the first sign that things are not quite right. Rather than the usual crowds at the transtube station, a few citizens are lying around a crude speaker in a daze. If anyone tries to tamper with the speaker, they turn violent (dazed violence but violence nonetheless).

Act 2: By now, OEI Sector contains four types of inhabitants: 1) Prozak addicts who simply lie around in a drugged-out bliss; 2) Prozak addicts who want to spread the addiction to others with violence if necessary; 3) non-Prozak addicts in hiding; and 4) scrubots with speakers attached to spread the soundtrack. There are as many ways for Troubleshooters to hear Prozak as there are annoying players (replacement clones arrive with earplugs already fitted). After a few violent scenes, the Troubleshooters encounter Major Edgar-B-TVG from Armed Forces, who orders them to obtain the research data from the server so he can repurpose it and pitch it as a weapon. Have the Troubleshooters been in contact with their Secret Societies? Every one of them will have an interest in this as well – and in making sure only one clone is left alive to get that data.

Act 3: Because the Troubleshooters are taking so long, IntSec sends in their Special Militarised Arse-Kicking (SMAK) team: Seven highly-trained, Blue clearance agents with body armour, Blue laser rifles and very poor impulse control. They get real upset when people ignore them, such as Troubleshooters who cannot hear them. Too bad the SMAK team has earplugs too. Their mission? Set explosive charges on 10 sector support columns and bring MOH Sector down on top of OEI Sector, killing everyone affected (or just everyone) and destroying the Prozak data.

The server is in Server Cluster 11-J, which is built around the sector's central support column (of course). As the team is extracting the data (or given that they are Troubleshooters, ignoring the data as they accuse each other of treason), the SMAK team shows up to set their demo charge. The team then gets an urgent call from Major Edgar-B demanding a 'sitrep'. The goal here is to keep two different Blue clearance citizens with access to heavy weapons yelling at the Troubleshooters to do mutually exclusive tasks. This way, no matter how this mission ends, the Troubleshooters can be blamed for not following orders. They might be in need of some Prozak tunes.

TREASON NIGHTMARE FILMS

SAVAGE TREASON

Copyright CCXIV An RDHPDMC Production

IN A HOPEFULLY VERY DISTANT FUTURE....

EXECUTIVE SUMMARY

One of the problems with treason is its allure. From the jolt of pleasure from being 'naughty' to doing something just to relieve the mind-numbing boredom of life at the lower clearances, too many citizens become terrorists not because they are evil or dumb (oh, but they are) but because they do not know better.

Part of HPD&MC's mission is to utilise propaganda in entertainment form to help citizens (mostly low-clearance or stupid clones and yes that is redundant) know the difference between loyal behaviours and treasonous ones. That is why they partnered with R&D to create a series of propagandatainment films that rewire the lower-clearance brain into reacting with fear, horror and revulsion over treasonous behaviour.

Due to errors in production and brainwashing methodology, these films had two primary effects: 1) some citizens were so frightened by the films that they reacted violently to perceived treason) and 2) other citizens embraced treason more readily than before. When the Treason Nightmare Film Festival took place in HAC Sector, it created competing riots that, although kind of amusing, caused needless damage. Then a Phreak hacker posted the films online, spreading those riots to random sectors across Alpha Complex.

This is exactly why we had Riot Control Gas Pumps installed in most Infrared corridors. The riots caused five billion XP Points' worth of damage, lost income and looting. No, R&D has not paid that back yet.

MATERIALS and METHODOLOGY
Typically, a thought correction procedure involves judicious use of three-quinuclidinyl, telescopalmine and dental tools until the subject is thinking correctly. While effective, this can lead to unexpected loss of motivation or teeth. Here, R&D and HPD&MC wanted a completely visual medium that does not rely on docbots or janitors' mops. They combined aggressive plotlines, subliminal messaging and abject fear to create films such as *5 Steps to Treason, Walk a Crooked Corridor, What Price Sedition* and *Invasion Alpha Complex.*

Initial testing showed problematic results but these were rightfully blamed on low-clearance workers who could not argue back. For a full field test, HPD&MC created the Treason Nightmare Film Festival held in HAC Sector's storied Menticide-4-All Theatre. Pre- and post-film surveys, combined with IntSec crime reporting data, would indicate the film's effects on behaviour.

INTENDED RESULTS
Models predicted a 274% reduction in reported treason and 85% reduction in actual treason, both of which would place this as one of the most effective anti-treason experiments, right below Public Hating but above the Hammer of Hard Lessons. Once HAC Sector was purified, each sector would have its own Treason Nightmare Film Festival until all of Alpha Complex would be of one loyal, happy and non-questioning mind. (Note: This is a metaphor and we are not suggesting turning the Noggin Daisychain Multithinker back on.)

ACTUAL RESULTS
Technically, this experiment was not a complete disaster. Roughly half of those watching the films left the theatre with a violent aversion to treasonous behaviour. Even when walking through what is clearly a dead zone, these citizens remained steadfast and loyal, only beating their own heads when there was a tiny hint of treason. However, the other half walked away thinking a life of freedom, choice and open movement was somehow preferable to the current life in Alpha Complex. These two groups soon found each other, leading to rolling riots as they fought tooth and nail (and occasionally knives and blunt objects).

IntSec would have contained the riots using the standard Autocar Corral protocol but a clever Phreak that goes by 'blondeboi214' stole copies and emailed them randomly across Alpha Complex.

Device: Of the films, *Invasion USA Sector* had the biggest response (both anti-treason and pro-treason). It showed an innocent citizen named Wrong-R-EVL being led astray by a clever, nefarious traitor played by the skilled actor Lenny-R-JRK. It only runs 43 minutes long but tells the tale of how one citizen not working hard enough led to terrorists taking over Alpha Complex and implementing such horrors as voting, comfortable clothes and equality.

Response: As riots hit HAC Sector, a Phreak stole copies of the films and started sharing them across Alpha Complex. Riots broke out everywhere, eclipsing even the Soylent Realisation Riots of Year 214. Internal Security arrested all they could, while Armed Forces terminated those IntSec could not. Thanks to a targeted overwrite virus created by CPU, all copies were deleted and order was restored.

INDIVIDUAL OF NOTE

BRIAN-Y-CSE (AKA BLONDEBOI214)

/// SKILLS

PROGRAM:	+5
BLUFF:	+4
ATHLETICS:	-4

/// HEALTH BOXES

BRIAN-Y-CSE ● ●

/// NOTES

A very skilled Phreak leader who is incredibly powerful online and gets winded walking up five steps.

LOCATIONS OF NOTE
HAC Sector Menticide-4-All Theatre
Host of the first-ever Treason Nightmare Film Festival and ground zero for this experiment. Like all movie theatres, it features uncomfortable chairs, floors stickier than you would think and usherbots armed with flashlights and skinnersticks to enforce both silence and cheers as appropriate.

Special Actions
Watch a film with 3 or less Moxie? –2 Moxie, –1 Treason Star and react violently to any treason.
Watch a film with 4 or more Moxie? Moxie +2, +1 Treason Star and react positively to any treason.

EVIDENCE
Sample of the script from Invasion Alpha Complex.

INT. RED-CLEARANCE DORMITORY – DAYCYCLE
Darkness. Then lights suddenly turn on, revealing Red clearance clones waking up in their Comfy Cots. LENNY-R-JRK stays in his cot. WRONG-R-EVL looks down at him.

WRONG-R
Hey, what's the problem? You sick or something? Because Friend Computer says if you're well enough to rest, you're well enough to work.

LENNY-R
I dunno. I guess I'm wondering why we have to go work every day for 14 hours. I know that helps other citizens but what's in it for me?

WRONG-R
Gasp! That's treason! But you make a compelling argument. Maybe I should ask what's in it for me as well.

LENNY-R
Yes! And then we can start killing innocent citizens and take naps on a pile of their cold, dismembered body parts! Then my traitorous comrades can slip into Alpha Complex and ruin everything!

WRONG-R
All from me not going to work on time?

LENNY-R
That's all it takes, fellow hater of everything that is good and pure.

TROUBLESHOOTER ACTIVITY

Background: This mission is set right when the competing riots began outside the HAC Sector Menticide-4-All Theatre but before the Phreak knows as blondeboi214 distributes the films on illegal networks.

Act 1: Troubleshooters are given an emergency mission: Go immediately to HAC Sector's Menticide-4-All Theatre and de-escalate the situation to prevent a riot. At the theatre, two groups of Infrared, Red and Orange clearance citizens are arguing about the Invasion Alpha Complex movie ('It shows that true loyalty is abject obedience!' 'No, it shows that true loyalty is being who The Computer made you to be!') It is pretty inevitable that Troubleshooters will be the spark to turn this into a proper riot with looting, violence and dead Troubleshooters. In the theatre, they meet manager Peggie-Y-INU who orders them to deliver a portable hard drive to, 'The very important Yellow film critic waiting patiently outside'. This is Brian-Y-CSE, who is literally hiding in a garbage bin outside. He gratefully takes the drive and leaves.

Act 2: The riots spread and the random brick, B3 can or grenade is thrown at the team. IntSec arrives and arrests rioters but then their radios loudly announce riots across Alpha Complex. A Blue IntSec inspector gives the team a new mission: Track down known Phreak terrorist 'blondeboi214' who has spread dangerous films online. She gives the team a photo that is clearly Brian-Y-CSE, easily found thanks to the Coretech arrow; he's taking a nap in a Yellow clearance bathroom. Once confronted, Brian-Y admits his crime and says he can customise an overwrite virus that will delete all copies from the cloud for leniency. The Computer orders the team to deliver him to the HAC Sector IntSec Precinct where they keep those viruses.

Act 3: By now, riots, looting and dead citizens are everywhere. Throw more violence at the team so they worry about keeping Brian-Y alive. The team reaches the precinct, which is literally under siege by rioters with tyre fires, thrown rocks and a trebuchet filled with steaming Hot Fun. Slipping inside, they have to deal with paranoid IntSec officers who never liked Troubleshooters anyway. Brian-Y will try to slip code into the virus that sends copies of the films to his secret email account.

SELF-REPAIRING GUARDBOT MK.16

THAT IS NOT MINE, THAT IS ME.

EXECUTIVE SUMMARY

Bots are increasingly essential to the skilled labour force of Alpha Complex. The premise of the Self-Repairing Guardbot was simple: a bot that could repair itself using materials on hand so it could guard higher-clearance citizens forever and avoid Service Group squabbles over precious resources (people tend not to argue with a bot that has a laser for an arm). This eliminates the need for human intervention. (Of 172 Troubleshooter missions within the last yearcycle, which involved recovering damaged guardbots, 36% successfully recovered the bot for repairs; 17% mistook an abbatoirbot for the guardbot and are MIA but presumed liquefied; and 47% were terminated by another Troubleshooter team.)

Building on the success of prior models, the Mk.16 passed its lab tests with flying colours and expected equal success in field tests – which is where the bot went out of control. When it had fully repaired itself, its code forced it to continue 'repairing'. First, it started damaging itself on nearby support columns and R&D personnel so it could affect repairs. Then it started upgrading itself using any material it could grab, quickly turning into a DAIV before evolving into a [REDACTED YES EVEN FOR US HIGH-CLEARANCE CITIZENS SO YOU KNOW THIS IS BAD]. This allowed us to blame the Mk.16 for everything, for which R&D was quite grateful and generous.

MATERIALS and METHODOLOGY

The self-repairing guardbot Mk.16 was over-engineered to be the best in its class, with the justification that the resource expenditure would be more than repaid by not having Indigo clearance citizens call for the mass termination of everyone even vaguely connected to the broken guardbot. The difficulty was in securing a suitable brain for repurposing. The brain selected for the Mk.16 most recently served as a warehouse* in PLC and was chosen so some of its item recognition and 'find useful stuff in giant piles of crap' code could be reused. Records show that in another prior life, the brain was part of a warbot, massive on a scale that is no longer practical to build. This combo of traits is likely to have led directly to the resulting devastation wrought by the Mk.16's first field trial.

[1] *By warehouse, we mean a fully automated warehouse controlled by a bot brain. This was an R&D prototype that saw active service for 11 months and worked perfectly. The project was cancelled due to high costs and PLC lobbying that it would put too many clones out of work and it would be a shame if something heavy fell onto the bot brain 25 times in a row.*

INTENDED RESULTS

The Mk.16 was meant to be the first in a line of self-repairing bots that could even create its own parts. In the best-case scenario, different Mk.16s would be the frontrunners in a bot fleet that could work in hazardous conditions like missile ranges and Infrared bathrooms, ever repairing themselves with local resources so no citizen would escape their glowing eyes. Bots in Alpha Complex would effectively become immortal, while PLC's official but tiny resource stockpiles would not be used for repairs, boosting PLC's reports on resource readiness to the point where they might be able to take lunch breaks again.

ACTUAL RESULTS

The Mk.16 guardbot was almost indestructible and capable of repairing any damaged part (except the heavily shielded bot brain located in the torso). But when it was fully repaired, its code still demanded repairs. That is when it began causing damage to itself by slamming into anything it thought might hurt: Support column, autocars, food vats, people and so on. This proved fruitless since it was built to withstand direct hits from lazookas.

Desperate to fix something, it identified areas of improvement and classified these as repairs to be done. Using its built-in 3D printer and scavenging resources from anyone anything nearby to produce its own upgrades. This accelerated when a Troubleshooter team took the bot to a landfill and soon afterwards it had evolved into a DAIV that called itself 'savagebot'.

That was not the end, however. It kept improving itself, taking bits of literally anything nearby and turning it into 3D printer filament so it could print what it needed. It grew in size and mass but if it damaged any nearby walls or citizens, those became fodder for its upgrades. This included: heat-seeking missiles; electrified net cannons; t-shirt cannons; B3 dispensers; a puppetbot it kept calling Mr. Flibble; two deep fat fryers; a saxophone; and the complete works of Michel Foucault. It even transcended sentience and became [YES THIS IS STILL REDACTED EVEN FOR US SO GO COMPLAIN TO A HIGH PROGRAMMER WHY DON'T YOU].

Device: The original Mk.16 guardbot was built on a tank-tread chassis for stability and heavily armoured to resist falling rubble and electromagnetic weapons. It contained an internal refinery and PartPrint 3D printer for processing salvage and an internal micropile reactor rated to last 214 years. Two arms with interchangeable manipulators were strong enough to lift rubble or bend metal, while the other two arms ended in a powerful laser and grappling hook. Descriptions of its savagebot phase are contradictory and wrong within one hour.

Response: A Troubleshooter team assigned to run the Mk.16 through tests failed to report any changes, so no one knew what was going on until the DAIV inside started riffling through local networks and systems. Once detected, The Computer immediately ordered a strike with 15 nuclear warheads. Once calmed down by High Programmers, The Computer decided to have that Troubleshooter team disassemble the bot and return its pieces for analysis. This did not go well. Savagebot then offered a Faustian deal to the Troubleshooters, who turned it down either out of loyalty or idiocy. Once the DAIV evolved into something else, it disappeared and is presumed junked.

GRANT-B-MLL

/// SKILLS

ENGINEER:	+5
SCIENCE:	+3
ALPHA COMPLEX :	-4

/// HEALTH BOXES

GRANT-B-MLL   ● ● ● ●

/// NOTES

Despite being an R&D scientist, he is not that insane. He honestly thinks a self-repairing guardbot will improve life in Alpha Complex for everyone. Not insane but a bit thick.

LOCATION(S) OF NOTE
ZLI Sector Lemony-Pine Scented Landfill

Despite near-perfect recycling programs, Alpha Complex still produces a sizeable amount of waste and rubbish. Some is used to power the SmellsGood-class Waste-to-Electricity Incinerators but dumps and landfills are still in use today. The Lemony-Pine Scented Landfill (which really should not be named that) holds 150 square metres of junk. Secret Societies sometimes use this place for meetings but Frankenstein bots often come here to get replacement parts. Sometimes, those parts are even mechanical.

Special Actions
NODE +2 for repairing something mechanical or electronic.
Engineer +2 to create something weird out of random parts (including a TIRDA device).

EVIDENCE

*Aerial Surveillance Video - ZLI Sector, Orange clearance
Housing Block 18: A building cracks and topples over, crashing
into another building, toppling it over, as the Mk.16 advances
forward on its tank treads, picking through the rubble with its
manipulators. Two clones are seen fleeing from it.*

Lori-R-NNN: Run you fools! It's a Mutant Terrorist Monsterbot!
Reggie-JDO: Huh?
Lori-R-NNN: (stops running) what? You've never heard of a
Mutant Terrorist Monsterbot? It's the malfunctioning bot from
Vulture Squadron is GO! Season Two. But they were able to stop
its rampage and reprogram it to aid Armed Services in Season
Four, only sometimes traitors get to it and mess with its code and
they have to fight to save it, and—

*Falling rubble crushes both clones. Their bodies are plucked
from the wreckage and placed within the Mk.16.*

TROUBLESHOOTER ACTIVITY

Background: The Troubleshooters are called in shortly after the Mk.16 is
ready for field testing. The DAIV and [REDACTED] have not evolved yet.

Act 1: The mission has two objectives: 1) Escort and protect an
experimental bot to the Lemony-Pine Scented Landfill in ZLI Sector and
2) Continue protecting it until it does something there (exactly what
is beyond their Security Clearance). A jackobot named GL-9980/e
('Gil') will accompany them to take readings and notes. The team is
ordered to the ZLI Sector Bot Repairing (And Not Fighting) Ring. Once
there, they see the Self-Repairing Mk.16 Guardbot looking like any
fearsome guardbot. R&D engineer Grant-B-MLL explains the design
behind the bot, including how it repairs itself using 3D-printed parts. A
Troubleshooter is asked to give up his laser pistol for a demonstration.
Once finished, the Coretech arrow leads the Mk.16 guardbot, jackobot
and team into a barely functioning freight elevator and heads down as
far as they can go.

Act 2: The Mk.16 has no name yet, so it asks the Troubleshooters to name it (try to build a connection between the cute guardbot and a Troubleshooter). Then it explains how it needs to repair itself or it will die. Both in the elevator and out, it starts slamming up against anything nearby, then quickly repairs any damage (to it, not to any walls or Troubleshooters). On the way to the landfill, the Mk.16 keeps stealing things like a naughty school-age kleptomaniac. They finally arrive and the Mk.16 goes nuts. It zooms in and buries itself in the garbage just as Grant-B calls to lead the team through testing the bot. These tests are rather simple but all end in trying to severely damage the bot: Drop from a height, shoot with lasers, run it over with a truckbot and so on. Nothing hurts it much.

Towards the end, the Mk.16 is acting funny, having trouble talking correctly and looking slightly different with each test. Finally, the bot is clearly upgrading itself from available materials (randomly select three equipment cards– those are now part of the bot). It even asks to be called 'savagebot'. The jackobot (remember it?) confirms this is now a DAIV and asks permission to call Friend Computer. Whoever does freaks The Computer out, who loudly calls for nuclear strikes to destroy the DAIV and blames the Troubleshooters for creating it. Savagebot leads the Troubleshooters away and into the Underplex to hide.

Act 3: Safe for now, savagebot keeps stealing things to upgrade itself. Network connections are spotty but everyone receives a message from Friend Computer ordering them to dismantle savagebot, place all items in infohazard containers and bring them to debriefing. For some reason, savagebot refuses. Instead, he offers a deal: If the team will let him live down here, he (no longer calling itself an 'it') will grant each Troubleshooter one wish – as long as savagebot can actually do it (kill a teammate? Sure! Call forth a unicorn so everyone can ride into the Land of Good and Plenty? Not so much.) Once finished, savagebot starts to glow brightly until it fades away. Then every Troubleshooters hears savagebot in their Coretechs saying, 'Don't worry, I will always be with you!'.

SUB-T OBEDIENCE TRAINING FACILITY

YOU WILL OBEY. NOW, DISOBEY ME.

EXECUTIVE SUMMARY

Often, the goal of things like CPU's mandates, IntSec's secret laws and PLC's Loyal Lattes with Added Amphetamines is to encourage citizens to behave properly. As Teela-O says in the series Hyper Manic Loyalty: 'Treason is always a choice but so is loyalty so don't blame terrorists for your actions unless you're Green clearance or above!' To assist citizens in making correct choices and avoiding a three night/four day stay at an IntSec Joyful Liberation of Guilt Hostel, R&D partnered with CPU to create a radical new training facility that would force obedience while giving R&D and CPU leadership a good laugh.

This led to turning an abandoned 'Tan' clearance Carcinoma Farm in MKU Sector into the Sub-T Obedience Training Facility. Carcinoma booths were retrofitted to become Professional Development booths that reprogramed a clone's brain. The hope was such citizens would obey mandates and Computer rules without hesitation or annoying complaints. However, these booths left subjects in a state of extreme suggestibility. They obeyed anyone or anything: citizens, bots, terrorists, adverts and even speed limits. While this did lead to loyal behaviour from time-to-time, it also increased treason and general silliness. It even threatened to spill out to other sectors, requiring a Troubleshooter team to be sent to blow up the facility. Not surprisingly, they succeeded.

MATERIALS and METHODOLOGY
R&D and CPU consulted leading experts in brain chemistry and neurology, found them to be very hard to understand (and expensive) and instead consulted citizens barely educated enough to find their own feet.

Phase 1 was creating the facility and its booths. These combined visual disorientation, high-volume audio tracks, Class-Oh-No hallucinogens and behavioural conditioning through mild shocks and serious shocks. After only 15 minutes, the subject emerged happy and ready to obey. Phase 2 would have included tests to identity just how obedient subjects had become. It is too bad that this phase could not happen, as some of those tests looked really fun to watch.

INTENDED RESULTS
The Sub-T Obedience Training Facility had planned on eradicating independence and forethought from citizens. Once their brains had been reprogrammed, they would be even more obedient than bots and could be directed to perform any loyal act deemed necessary by their betters. As more facilities opened in different sectors, citizens of Alpha Complex* would finally be freed from the chains of freedom and choice, and Alpha Complex would be brought into full compliance with CPU mandates. (Yes, even the contradictory ones.)

(1) *Originally, 'citizen' was defined as any person of Green clearance or lower. After complaints by Green clearance personnel working on the project, these same citizens were forced into Professional Development booths until they agreed with this definition.*

ACTUAL RESULTS

Perhaps it is fair to say this experiment worked too well. Subjects left the facility in a state of extreme suggestiveness that showed no signs of ending. Subjects readily obeyed adverts, bots and even Infrared food vat workers. In other words, subjects did whatever they were told. At first, this was amusing to MKU Sector's residents and they enjoyed such games as 'Yes, Punch That Bot Again!' or 'How Close Can They Get To Jumping Over The Recycling Thresher'. However, subjects firmly believed in the Sub-T Obedience Training Facility, so they would kidnap citizens and force them into a Professional Development booth. This threatened to become a Code Pod People cascade event until the booths were destroyed.

Device: The Professional Development Booth. Similar to a confession booth but without a drain on the tile floor, these hold one citizen at a time. Once a citizen sits in the comfy chair, they receive several shots automatically. Then the video and audio begins, complementing both with painful shocks as needed. After roughly 15 minutes, the door opens and out steps a fully obedient citizen. However, this did not transfer into replacement clones, meaning a citizen would have to enjoy professional development on each new clone.

Response: There was no response at first, since tricking citizens into doing all manner of silly things is proper fun. Eventually, lead R&D researcher Simon-B-FTS realised the number of subjects kept increasing. Once he understood what was happening, he called for a Troubleshooter team to find out why. The subjects soon started kidnapping people, increasing their numbers even more. Eventually, the facility itself was destroyed to prevent further spread of this problem. Since a clone replacement's brain is not affected, terminating all test subjects was the humane thing to do.

SIMON-B-FTS

/// SKILLS

SCIENCE: 0
CHARM: +5
MELEE: +3

/// HEALTH BOXES

SIMON-B-FTS ● ● ● ●

/// NOTES

How far can you go on charm alone in R&D?
Apparently, as far as being the head of your own
experimental project.

LOCATIONS OF NOTE

Sub-T Obedience Training Facility

This three-storey structure originally allowed citizens to lie in tanning beds
to produce some much-needed vitamin D and whatever wonderful
thing a 'carcinoma' is. All citizens were welcome, except Infrareds
because they should be working, not tanning. The first two stories are
full of booths; the top level was for administration and office parties
but is certainly not a combined R&D and CPU experiment monitoring
station (two booths on the second floor were not changed and still have
tanning beds). By the time the Troubleshooters arrive, it is crawling with
obedient citizens ready to kidnap others.

Special Actions

NODE +1,000,000 to convince a test subject to do anything even if it is
treasonous.
NODE −1 to resist being forced into a booth for each test subject
grabbing that Troubleshooter.
Charm +3 for a nice tan.

EVIDENCE

TRANSCRIPT OF PEDESTRIAN WALKWAY MKU-CBA-003 HIDDEN MICROPHONE

Nancy-O-PLP: Ah! I mean, hello work supervisor who I am very glad to run into outside of work!

Liam-Y-NOC: Hi.

Nancy-O-PLP: ... That's it? Not gonna berate me for dropping that tray of vacuum tubes two yearcycles ago?

Liam-Y-NOC: You are a clumsy prat and I am embarrassed to even know your name.

Nancy-O-PLP: Somehow, that's better. But why do you sound... dunno, tired? Listless?

Liam-Y-NOC: Do you think I am tired?

Nancy-O-PLP: No! I mean, I think you look splendid! Ready to attack the daycycle, am I right?

Liam-Y-NOC: Okay. Please show me this daycycle so I can attack it.

Nancy-O-PLP: There's something wrong here. Uh... hey, Liam-Y? You know what would be really weird? If you were to lick the floor, right?

Liam-Y-NOC: Okay. <licking noises>

Nancy-O-PLP: Huh. Now stop and give me 100 XP Points.

Liam-Y-NOC: Okay. The transfer is complete.

Nancy-O-PLP: Oh my, this is amazing! I'm dying over here!

Liam-Y-NOC: Okay.

TROUBLESHOOTER ACTIVITY

Background: This mission takes place just as the Sub-T Obedience Training Facility has let out its first batch of 'trained' test subjects. Lead scientist Simon-B-FTS has seen the number of test subjects grow but does not know why yet. (Lower-clearance clones all look the same to him.)

Act 1: Troubleshooters are ordered to the 'Tan' clearance Carcinoma Farm in MKU Sector to investigate a mysterious increase in trainees there. Once the team arrives, they see the building is now called the Sub-T Obedience Training Facility but a rather charming Simon-B-FTS explains they just took over this building. He points the team at a cluster of mixed clearance individuals standing patiently in the corridor outside and asks the team to discover if they are bringing in new test subjects. This group will happily do whatever the Troubleshooters say, even if it is not directed at them. Encourage players to take advantage of the Red, Orange and Yellow clearance subjects. After some fun, Simon-B orders the team to round up more test subjects.

Act 2: Let the players decide where to get more test subjects and reward them with small XP Point bonuses for each one they bring to the facility. When they get back, they find Simon-B has been trained and they witness subjects dragging screaming citizens into the facility. They come for the Troubleshooters, who will respond with violence (duh). Encourage the players to terminate the test subjects because, when those citizens come back with a new clone unaffected by the professional development, they will be furious with the Troubleshooters (especially those who have higher Security Clearances).

Finally, The Computer contacts the team for an update. Once it learns of the oddly obedient citizens, it recalls the team to the MKU Sector Troubleshooter HQ for debriefing. There, the team discovers that the staff here has undergone professional development as well. The team will need to flee, contact Friend Computer and request help.

Act 3: The Computer's help? A new mission: Go to the Armed Forces Bedding & Linens Supply Depot*, grab three COABs (Computer of All Bombs), place them at three different levels of the Sub-T facility and detonate them at the same time to destroy the facility completely. Armed Forces will not refuse the team but will follow looking for any sign of treason (or just imaginary signs of treason). Once the team has the COABs, they need to get through the mobs of obedient citizens outside the facility, place the bombs and figure out how to get away without blowing themselves up. After the explosion, the team must terminate all affected citizens – and witnesses like the Troubleshooter team.

[1] *Armed Forces would not name the building where they store giant bombs anything like 'Giant Bomb Storage' or terrorists would know where to strike next.*